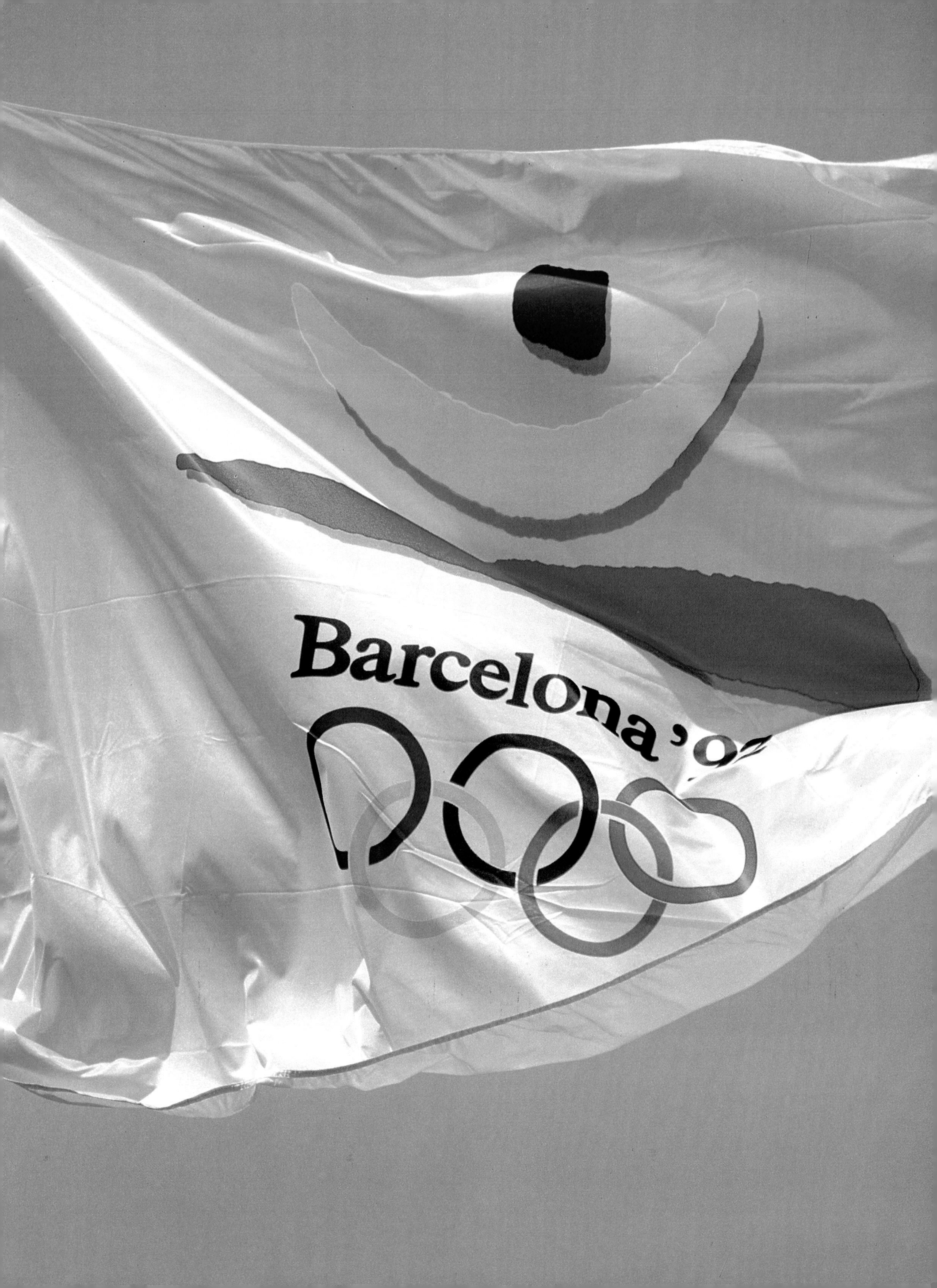
Barcelona '92

THE COMMEMORATIVE BOOK OF BARCELONA '92

C O N T E N T S

I t was at the 91st session of the International Olympic Committee on 17th October 1986 in Lausanne that Barcelona was awarded the honour of staging the XXVth Olympiad.

I can say today, as President of the International Olympic Committee, that the Games this year were a resounding success; not only because all the most experienced athletes were present, accompanied by their National Olympic Committees, but also because these athletes gave their absolute best, to our great satisfaction. Of course, the organisation was also a success, for everything in Barcelona and its surrounding area was prepared, renovated, extended or specially constructed in order to ensure a magnificent reception for the participants, spectators and television viewers from all over the world.

For 16 days, our hearts were stirred as more than 10,000 athletes from 5 continents provided us with a wonderful and splendid example of Olympic fraternity.

In the name of the Olympic movement and all sports, I should like once again to congratulate the Organising Committee and its President, Pasqual Maragall, and express my heartfelt thanks. Their tremendous work and that of the 102.000 volunteers merit praise of the highest order.

This book offers a day-by-day visual account of the Games in all their glory. Its superb pictures shall never fade from the memories of those who experienced the Games first hand. And I hope that they will allow others an insight into the emotion that coursed through these Games.

Juan Antonio Samaranch
President of the IOC

As unavoidable as the afternoon sun, Barcelona provided
a constant reminder that, while the world might well have
considered the Olympics a temporary property of Spain,
the Games also belonged to the people of Catalonia.

CATALONIA'S GAMES

The original planners of Barcelona built a city that resembled a fortress. Though many of the ancient walls remain, Barcelona became open to inspection by the world as host of the XXV Olympiad in 1992. And while the 500,000 who visited surely were impressed by the city's new sports facilities, it is the cultural vibrance of this Mediterranean port that will linger in their memories.

Despite Madrid's reputation as the cosmopolitan jewel of Spain, Barcelona and its Catalonian heritage, captivating architecture, and distinctly European pulse made it the ideal venue for the intoxicating mix of people and languages assembled for the Olympic Games. A city populated by 1.7 million residents, Barcelona is no stranger to congested streets and subways, long taxi lines and crowded cafes.

In contrast to the typical, however, was the new face of Barcelona that took shape in the years leading to the Games, most notably a revived waterfront, miles of restored beaches and a more expansive highway system. About $8 billion was invested in construction projects inspired by the Olympics, thus bringing about the most substantial civic renewal in European history.

"Part of the benefit of the Olympic movement is that people visit cities at the best possible time," said Barcelona mayor Pasqual Maragall.

This appetite for progress, as demonstrated by the many giant construction cranes dotting Barcelona's cityscape, has not overshadowed the essence of the Catalonian capital—architecture. As an example, first-time visitors are still marveling at the detail and magnitude of the famous Sacred Family Church, a project initiated in 1891 by the adventurous Antoni Gaudi. The towering cathedral in the city's Eixample district is a monument to architecture of the Modernist era, and to patience. More than 100 years after Gaudi started, the cathedral remains unfinished.

Tourists who sought a break from arenas and stadiums during the Games might have found refuge inside Barcelona's numerous museums. Four of Spain's most renowned artists – Josep Clara, Pablo Picasso, Joan Miro and Antoni Tapies – are celebrated in buildings dedicated exclusively to their work.

Eating also classifies as art in Barcelona, particularly in Catalan restaurants such as La Odisea (the "Spago of Spain"), trendy, found in the city's Gothic Quarter, or in chic, ultramodern establishments where the decor and the prices make equally lasting impressions. Even the smallest neighborhood taverns, or tapas bars, offer a pleasant diversion from the predictible.

Regardless of preferences for art, architecture or food, every visitor must soon adjust to a strictly observed pace of life. Lunch is not limited to nutrition. Indeed, it is a welcome break from the snarled traffic circles and relentless stream of motorbikes. Dining is a late-night phenomenon followed by a quick transition to clubs and outdoor cafes, or long walks along Las Ramblas, a street dominated by people watching, dueling vendors and cocktails.

Barcelona: "A unique city of unparalleled beauty." Miguel de Cervantes.

A devil of a night-life! 250 leisure areas and 1200 clubs.

The focal point of activity during the Games was Montjuic Park, home of the Olympic Stadium built originally in 1929, but returned to its former splendor following massive renovation. The 65,000-seat stadium hosted the opening ceremonies and later welcomed the world's track and field fans.

Next door is the 17,000-seat Palau Sant Jordi, a facility inspired by Japanese architecture that rates among the best indoor arenas in Olympic history. Montjuic was host to many of the Games' marquee sports, including gymnastics, swimming and track and field which meant a constant stream of spectators from morning until late evening. To accomodate the crowds, a network of escalators was constructed, transporting 27,000 spectators every hour. After arriving at the top of Montjuic, visitors were afforded a spectacular view of the fountains in and around the busy Plaza d'España.

As unavoidable as the afternoon sun, Barcelona provided a constant reminder that, while the world might well have considered the Olympics a temporary property of Spain, the Games also belonged to the people of Catalonia.

Catalonia is an autonomously governed region of northeastern Spain. The culture has its roots in the Roman occupation of the area for six centuries, ending in the 5th Century A.D. Many of Barcelona's residents consider Spanish a second language, preferring to communicate in their native tongue, Catalan.

The Olympics were viewed as a particularly important forum through which to promote global awareness of the Catalonian struggle for independence, especially since International Olympic Committee president Juan Antonio Samaranch is a native of Barcelona and the region.

Josep Miquel Abad, chief executive officer of the Barcelona Olympic Organizing Committee (COOB), is only modestly diplomatic in his characterization of Catalonia as "the driving force behind the Barcelona candidature".

Indeed, the International Olympic Committee agreed to recognize the region's language as an "official" tongue during the Games, along with Spanish, English and French. Some six million people speak Catalan throughout Spain.

Regional fervor to heighten the cry for independence picked up immediately upon the death of General Francisco Franco in 1975. During Franco's 40-year dictatorship, the speaking of Catalan was forbidden and the region's autonomy was abolished from statutes.

The Olympic Games provided global awareness of Catalonia on a grand scale and underscored the marvelous diversity of Spain and its people.

Barcelona has always fought to reach the futur first. The names of Gaudì, Picasso, Dalì and Mirò speak volumes for the genius of its architects, sculptors and artists.

Page 12-13
Opposite the National Palace
the celebrations begin!

The Mirò Foundation.

The Casa Mila.

Homage to Miró.

Telecommunications tower of Montjuich, work of the architect Santiago Calatrava.

The Sagrada Familia, immediately recognizable symbol of the city.

AMERICAN ATHLETES

Although the vaunted basketball Dream Team lived up to
all expectations and three world records were toppled in
track and field, there were some agonizing setbacks in
boxing and gymnastics. By the closing ceremony,
American athletes had distinguished themselves with a
lofty total of 108 medals.

THE U.S. TEAM AT BARCELONA

Mike Powell, the humbled long jumper, never imagined that he would be cherishing a silver medal at the 1992 Summer Olympic Games. But that was precisely his state of mind as the Games of Barcelona neared their conclusion.

"It has been a weird Olympics," said Powell, the U.S. star and world recordholder who was second to Carl Lewis in the long jump final. "I don't know why. If I could put my finger on it, I'd have figured it out before I started. But, hey, at least I got a medal."

The unexpected was the norm for the U.S. Olympic Team during the XXVth Olympiad, but not because the Americans collected medals at a steady, deliberate pace. That happens every four years. It was how the final medal total of 108 was achieved that broke so decisively with tradition.

In team sports, the U.S. was foiled again and again. The exception, a highly regarded and unprecedented men's basketball Dream Team, easily fulfilled its considerable potential, but others expected to contend for gold medals encountered setbacks.

The women's basketball team, loaded with experience and past Olympians, was eliminated by the Unified Team in the semifinals and denied a chance to defend its 1984 and 1988 Olympic titles. The Dreamettes settled for a bronze medal, defeating Cuba in the third-place game 88-74.

"I know we came here and gave a complete effort," said team member Medina Dixon. "So I don't really know if I'm disappointed. I do know that I am frustrated. But we are going home with something. Even though it's the bronze, it's better than nothing."

Still, U.S. assistant coach Lin Dunn did not view the

The Dream Team on the gold medal podium. Sometimes the expected happens at the Olympics.

The US team, the largest of the Games with 1,049 athletes, coaches, and trainers, marches into Olympic Stadium.

tournament's outcome as altering her contention that the American team is the most talented group ever assembled. And player Teresa Edwards wasn't going home to sulk, she said, because "you can't let 40 minutes of poor shooting (against the Unified Team) ruin the rest of your life."

Similar reflection followed the men's volleyball team on its journey home from Barcelona. This team also arrived in Barcelona on a mission to win a third consecutive Olympic gold medal for the U.S., and was favored – along with Italy – to achieve that goal. But Brazil dashed that possibility in the semifinals, scoring a 3-1 victory and forcing the U.S. into a third-place game that was never in the game plan.

"Everyone thought that Italy would walk through this tournament," said the USA's Steve Timmons. "This is one of the most competitive, if not THE most competitive, tournaments I've ever played in during my life. The dream for a third is over and it hurts."

Third, as it turned out, would have been sweet consolation for Team USA in baseball. But there was to be no medal for the U.S., which had won the 1988 baseball title in Seoul before baseball gained medal status in the Games. Coach Ron Fraser and his 1992 edition were turned back in the bronze medal final by Japan, an 8-3 winner.

The baseball team began its Olympic journey with three consecutive wins and enough momentum to take a 5-0 lead in the first inning of Game 4 against rival and world baseball power Cuba. Quickly, the bubble burst, and Cuba came back to win a 9-6 victory from which the U.S. would never quite recover. The USA's loss to Japan for the bronze also marked the end of Fraser's 32-year coaching career, and it was not the final chapter he would have written if given the chance.

"It hasn't really settled in yet that this will be the last game," he would say. "I've been with amateur and international baseball for three decades and the most exciting time for me was when they announced baseball would be a full medal Olympic sport."

Mike Powell dueled with Carl Lewis long into the night.

Gail Devers stakes her claim to the title of world's fastest female.

Go USA!

The bizarre odyssey that defined the USA's Olympic experience was no less apparent among competitors in individual events, where the anticipation of glory was bluntly replaced by the hollowness of disappointment. It happened to four-time world champion Eric Griffin in boxing ... to world champion gymnast Kim Zmeskal ... to swimmer Matt Biondi ... to decathlete Dave Johnson, wrestler Kenny Monday, sprinter Michael Johnson, and tennis star Jim Courier.

Griffin, the gold medal favorite in the 106-pound division, was eliminated early in the Olympic boxing tournament against lightly regarded Rafael Lozano of Spain. Using a new electronic scoring system, the judges generated a final score that stunned most observers – 6-5, Lozano.

Despite registering far more scoring blows, Griffin did not receive all of the points he thought he earned because the new system requires three of the five judges to

Mike Barrowman on his way to gold in the 200m breaststroke.

acknowledge a legal blow within one second. They do this by punching a button on a control panel.

Griffin would lose his appeal to the International Amateur Boxing Association and call it the "worst decision I ever got". Indeed, the Griffin-Lozano bout will be counted among the most controversial bouts in Olympic history.

"I feel bad for some of my teammates because they got robbed by the system," said lightweight gold medalist Oscar De La Hoya. "They ought to go back to the old system, using pencil and paper."

While Shannon Miller would win five gymnastics medals for the U.S., the most coveted a silver in the all-around competition, her teammate Zmeskal endured the toughest few days of her accomplished career. Her collapse reached its pinnacle in the all-around, where Zmeskal ended up

10th. She made mistakes and suffered breaks in confidence to which Zmeskal had always appeared immune.

Her coach, Bela Karolyi, watched helplessly and became frustrated when none of his inspirational tactics seemed capable of turning his student around. The experience was so demoralizing that Karolyi announced he would retire when the Games concluded, although only time will tell if the veteran teacher – molder of Olympic champions Nadia Comaneci and Mary Lou Retton – can make a clean break from the sport.

Miller's success was not to be overshadowed, however. The fragile but determined youngster from Edmond, Oklahoma, exceeded every reasonable expectation in battling for second place in the all-around and helping the USA win a team bronze medal. She picked up three other

The Magic Man. A face as familiar in Barcelona as it is in the USA.

Shades of Jesse Owens.

Jackie Joyner-Kersee faltered in the shot put event, but still managed to win gold in the heptathlon.

medals in the individual apparatus events and her coach, Steve Nunno, later characterized Miller's collective effort as the finest Olympic performance ever by a U.S. gymnast.

Although Trent Dimas earned the first U.S. gold in men's gymnastics since 1984 — winning the horizontal bar event — the men's team placed sixth after arriving in Barcelona with hopes for a bronze medal.

"Maybe not training the kids hard enough is what we did wrong," U.S. coach Francis Allen said in the end. "We've got to do what the Russians are doing. They work them to death and, when they get to be 14 years old, they're strong. We do it different. We say, hey, if you make the Olympic team, great."

In swimming, it was not so much training technique as the passage of time that foiled Olympic champions Janet

Evans in the 400 freestyle and Matt Biondi in the 50 and 100 freestyles. Evans ultimately took the sting out of a silver-medal finish in the 400 by bouncing back to defend her 800 title. Biondi was a non-factor in the 100, placing fifth, while being upstaged in the 50 and earning a silver medal.

But as old heroes step aside for new stars, the U.S. kept churning right along in the Olympic swimming pool, picking up 27 medals, including 11 gold.

"In some ways," Evans would say, "this Olympics was the most satisfying. In Seoul, my success came very easy. It meant a lot to be able to hang on another four years."

It surely meant something to the good-natured Dave Johnson, since he hung on just long enough to finish the grueling two-day competition with a bronze medal dangling

A bright spot for the men's gymnastics team, Trent Dimas, a gold medal winner on the horizontal bar.

Page 23
World champion Kim Zmeskal fell short of high expectations, but helped her team win a bronze.

More often than not, this kind of determination paid off in victory on the track for the USA. Kevin Young shattered the world record in the 400-meter hurdles, winning in 46.78 seconds. Carl Lewis, a non-qualifier for the 100 meters, nonetheless raised his career gold medal total to eight, upstaging Powell in the long jump and claiming the title on his first attempt. He then anchored the 400-meter relay team as a late addition, helping it achieve a world record of 37.40 seconds. Gail Devers, crippled by Graves' Disease and subsequent medical complications in 1991, won the women's 100 meters and tearfully rejoiced in her miracle comeback.

"For me," Lewis said, "it was the best ever." Refering to his three relay partners, he added, "When you have a "dream team" in front of you, it's easy."

Easy would be an understatement in describing the road taken to the gold medal podium by the most celebrated basketball team of all time. They might have been justifiably called the Dream Team, but their opponents found out all too well that this squad's total dominance was real. And so were the smiles across their faces when, for a few moments, they were no longer millionaire celebrities with appointments to keep and golf tournaments to attend. As the American flag rose toward the ceiling and their national anthem played, Bird and Ewing, Jordan and Magic, Drexler and Barkley, and all the rest, were proud, victorious Olympians, plain and simple.

"It's a feeling you can't explain when you're on that stand," Michael Jordan of the Chicago Bulls said after the USA's 117-85 gold-medal victory against Croatia.

"The thing I'll remember when I'm older is that I once played alongside the best players who've ever played the game."

from his neck. While the U.S. track and field team was largely successful in Barcelona, winning 30 medals and accounting for three world records, Johnson was one of the hard-luck stories of the Games. He suffered a mild stress fracture during one of his final workouts and was ninth after Day 1 of the decathlon, facing the possibility that he would sink from medal contender to also-ran.

But Johnson recovered despite the pain in his ankle and came up with a bronze medal, fortunate that he even reached the finish of the final event, the 1,500 meters. "It took a lot of heart and prayer to get through," Johnson said.

The U.S. water polo team started off strong but lost momentum in the final matches.

Page 24-25
Tom Jager is 50 meters away from a bronze medal.

Pablo Morales did not make the U.S. team in 1988, but returned to Barcelona to bring back a pair of gold medals.

Eric Namesnik won a silver medal in the 400m medley.

Kristen Babb-Sprague, America's gold medal winner in synchronized swimming.

Page 27
Janie Wagstaff backstrokes for the U.S.

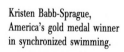

Mary Clark takes the bronze
in platform diving.

Page 30
Karen Laface on the
springboard. She faced tough
competition from the Chinese
divers.

Scott Donie demonstrates
form that won a silver medal
for the USA.

Page 28-29
American twins Karen and
Sarah Josephson claimed the
duet title and an American
sweep in synchronized
swimming.

Carlette Guidry receives the baton in the 4×100 relay. American relay teams won 3 out of 4 track relays.

Page 33
Carl Lewis successfully defends his Olympic long jump title. His first jump was the longest of the evening.

4×100 relay action. Another world record for the USA!

Jackie clears the bar on way to unprecedented repeat of Olympic heptathlon title.

Steve Lewis rounds a curve for the world record-breaking 4x100m relay team.

Kevin Young celebrates a world record in the 400m hurdles.

Carl Schueler and Marco Evoniuk in the 50km walk.

Page 37
Young is first to break the 47 second barrier in the 400m hurdles.

Stop showing off, Michael.

Katrina McClain jumps against Czechoslovakia. The Americans, upset by the Unified Team, took home the bronze.

«Maybe we could use this guy in the NBA.»

Page 38
Americans go for a rebound.

Dante Washington dribbles upfield. The USA lost the match to a powerful squad from Italy, 2-1.

The USA could not repeat their Olympic title in volleyball, but they did bring home a bronze medal.

Karyn Palgut gets off a shot in handball. The USA finished 6th in the event.

Calvin Murray takes a rip
against Japan. The Americans
did not medal in their
national pastime.

Lightweight Oscar De La
Hoya captured the only
boxing gold for the USA.

Chris Campbell has his opponent in a predicament. Chris finished the wrestling tournament with a bronze medal.

Kate Donahoo in Judo action against a Cuban opponent.

Page 44-45
Mary Jo and Gigi Fernandez won doubles gold in Tennis. Jennifer Capriati also took singles honors for the U.S. women.

Randy Smyth and Keith Notary sailed to one of 9 American medals in Olympic yachting.

Action in the kayaking (K-1) final. Greg Barton paddled to a bronze medal for the USA.

Carol Lavell riding the gelding Gifted. The U.S. team managed only one Equestrian medal, a bronze in individual jumping.

Skeet shooter Matt Dryke won a gold in 1984, but failed to medal at Barcelona.

Page 47
The Americans finished out of medal contention in the 100k team time trials.

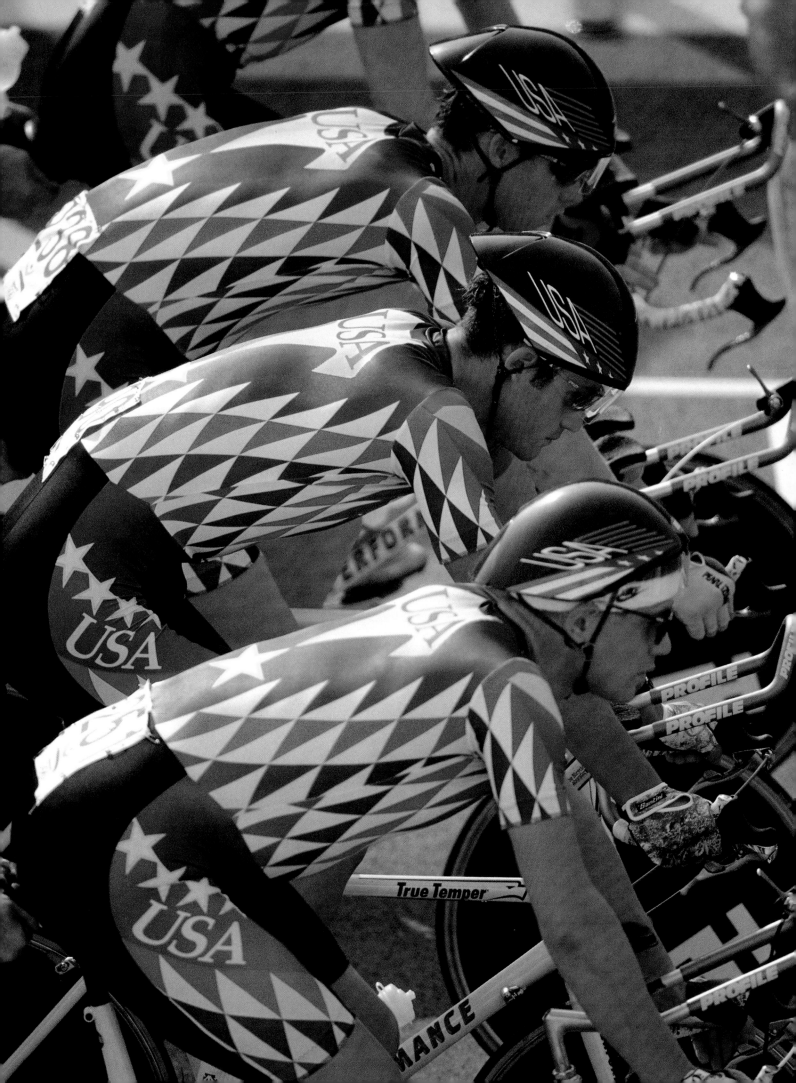

DAY

Under a clear Barcelona sky, it's a new dawning for the
Olympic Games, and a party for the world's newest
generation of athletic heroes.

THE GAMES BEGIN

The participants of the huge ceremony are dressed in the colors of the Barcelona'92 logo: red, blue and yellow, the colors of the Mediterranean.

The vows of fraternity among nations bring the opening ceremony to a moving close.

A crowd exceeding 65,000 jammed the Olympic Stadium on Montjuic to witness the expected festival of art and sport that defines the choreographed extravagance of an Opening Ceremony. But it was the unexpected that made possible an unforgettable climax to this dawning of the 1992 Games.

Antonio Rebollo, a 37-year-old archer, calmly fired an arrow into the darkness of a comfortable Barcelona evening, the arrow's tip transporting the cherished Olympic flame. With cool precision, Rebollo's shot rose into the sky on a perfect course toward the caldron that guards the symbolic flame. In a flash, the magical arrow cleared the caldron's rim and the audience erupted in applause.

There would be no second chance for Rebollo and his incredible performance under pressure will stand forever as an enduring Olympic memory.

The evening was made memorable by a number of historic moments, including the arrival of a South African delegation at an Olympic opening for the first time in 32 years and the procession of a United States delegation that was partially comprised of celebrity members of the USA's Dream Team basketball squad.

South Africa's Olympic flag was carried proudly by Jan Tau, a black marathoner and sports instructor who was born in 1960, the last year in which athletes from his country had appeared in the Games. The sports world had turned against South Africa by the mid-1960s, protesting the nation's segregated culture that was based on the legal pillars of apartheid. By 1970, the International Olympic Committee had formally banned South Africa from the Games. Now, at last, apartheid had been dismantled and the country's isolated athletes were on display for the world.

For the first time in the history of the Games, a flaming arrow lights up the Olympic bowl.

Terrifying monsters attack the ship.

"My dream was always to run against the best in the world," Tau was saying before the opening. "I was always praying that the officials would get us here someday."

"But I don't want to be involved in politics. I don't even consider it in my mind."

Following South Africa's arrival, the seemingly endless march continued: The first team from a united Germany since 1964; a festively attired delegation from Canada; the imposing athletes of the People's Republic of China, including several astonishingly tall females; the unified team representing 12 former republics of the Soviet Union, complete with a flag from each; the debut of teams from Croatia, Slovenia and the tiny nation of Namibia; and the newly named delegation from the Czech and Slovak Federative Republic.

The evening's procession of about 15,000 athletes and officials from 170 nations was further highlighted by the appearance of a team from the breakaway republic of Bosnia-Herzegovina, formerly a part of Yugoslavia. Only a week earlier, this 18-member delegation had no assurance of being in Barcelona representing their newly recognized country. But, on this night, for a brief, happy moment, politics and despair were put aside in the grandest of Olympic traditions.

With similar pride, newly recognized teams marched past from Croatia, Slovenia, Lithuania, Latvia and Estonia as the new world order went on display with vivid clarity.

Amid the excitement this evening stood a smiling Earvin "Magic" Johnson, the retired star of the USA's National Basketball Association and member of the Olympic Team. His enormous popularity around the world was never more apparent, as athletes from dozens of marching delegations paused to take his photograph or exchange friendly gestures. Athletes from Brazil, China and Central Africa even challenged security personnel, risking a brisk shove for the chance to snap a photo or get a quick glimpse of this adored superstar.

Later, the crowd's attention was directed to the final delegation – the team from Spain. Led by flagbearer Prince Felipe de Borbon, an Olympic yachtsman, the team moved in tight formation to its place on the stadium infield, engulfed by the applause and cheers of its countrymen.

IOC President Juan Antonio Samaranch addressed the huge crowd and a global television audience projected at 3.5 billion: "On behalf of the Olympic movement, of which I have the honor of being president, and personally, as a citizen of Barcelona, I would like to thank all the people who have contributed to this historic day."

King Juan Carlos of Spain rose from his box seat and with a brief pronouncement declared the Games of the XXV Olympiad open, and the anticipation turned to Antonio Rebollo's arrow, its flight of fancy carrying the hopes and dreams of a generation.

The castels or human towers symbolize the triumph of human will-power.

Cristina Hoyos among 200
bailaoras de flamenco.

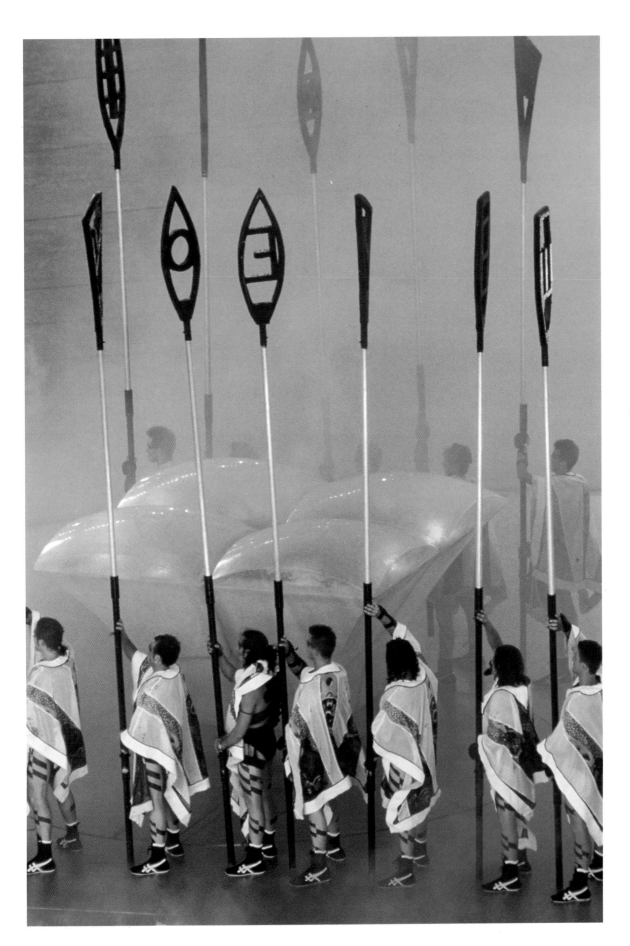

The legend of the Hercules enacted before 65,000 spectators.

We are welcomed by flowers and birds, symbols of peace. HOLA!

Page 56-57
The Mediterranean: Olympic sea and cradle of Latin civilization.

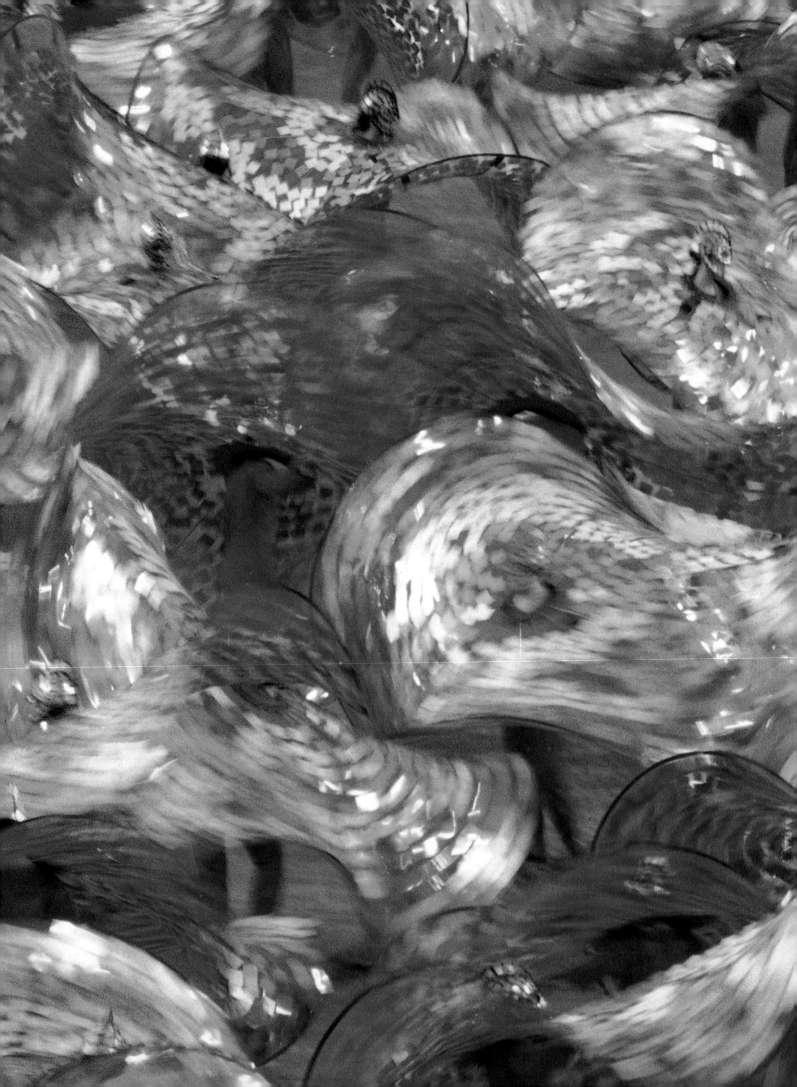

DAY

*The Dream Team debuts with an expected men's
basketball rout of Angola; South Africans make history,
ending three decades of Olympic exile.*

THE IMPOSSIBLE IS
REALITY FOR SOUTH AFRICA

Page 58
The first gold medal for the German team in the 100km cycle race.

The team from the Central African Republic places 29th.

A South Korean shooter competing in the women's air rifle event won the first gold medal of the se Olympic Games, but it was the shooters from the United States men's basketball team who stole the day and took their first step toward an Olympic title already awarded them by acclamation.

USA's 116-48 victory against overmatched Angola was, as anticipated, a poor impersonation of a basketball game. USA forward Charles Barkley, rarely accused of being a diplomat, kept the contest interesting with his physical style of play. Still, his decision to elbow an Angolan opponent drew whistles and boos from the crowd.

Over at the boxing arena, where hitting an opponent is less controversial, Fana Thwala became the first black South African to compete in an Olympic event a few hours after Trevor Strydom, a white modern pentathlete, achieved another milestone. Just before 10:00 a.m., Strydom met an opponent from Canada in the fencing phase of the modern pentathlon and thus emerged as the first South African of any color to appear in an Olympic competition in 32 years. The South Africans had been banned formally from the Games since 1970, but had yielded to political pressure and by-passed the 1964 and 1968 Games too.

"This is the start of a great future for our country," Strydom said.

And Thwala's coach Dan Bushney noted the significance as well, saying, "For our boxer, for our sport, for our country, this is a start. At this stage, its not winning a medal, its competing and trying your best."

At the swimming venue, China pulled off the major upset of the day when Yong Zhuang, 19, won the womens 100-meter freestyle gold medal at the expense of world recordholder Jenny Thompson of the USA. Zhuang, swimming the race faster than ever before in her career, established an Olympic record of 54.64 seconds. Thompson was second.

Despite her victory, Zhuang was later forced to defend herself against persistent claims within the international swimming community that China's top competitors have experimented with banned anabolic steroids in training.

"Many journalists and people claim we are doping," she would say. "But it is completely wrong. There is absolutely no scientific basis for it."

The first cycling gold medal of the Games was awarded to Germany, which upstaged a world champion Italian team in the 100-kilometer time trial. Bernd Dittert, Christian Meyer, Uwe Peschel and Michael Rich overcame Italy's 14-second lead at the trial's halfway mark to win by precisely one minute. France won the bronze, just ahead of a team from the Commonwealth of Independent States. This event was briefly disrupted when two members of the Swedish team sustained severe cuts after taking a violent spill.

Sadness visited the entire USA swim team before the day's first race when it was learned that the father of 200-meter individual medley qualifier Ron Karnaugh had died overnight. Peter Karnaugh, 60, suffered a heart attack during Saturday night's opening ceremony and was pronounced dead several hours later.

Peter Karnaugh and his wife, Jean, had decided to attend the Games after fans of their son's swimming career back home in Maplewood, N.J., had raised funds to pay for the trip. A little more than 30 minutes after Ron and his USA teammates had marched into the Olympic Stadium, smiling and waving to the crowd, Peter Karnaugh collapsed and was taken to a hospital.

USA vs. Angola: USA wins 116 to 48.

The Hungarian swimmer Krisztina Egerszegi sets a new Olympic record in the 400m medley.

Two weightlifting titles were decided on Day 3. South Korea's Chun Byung-Kwan established an Olympic record in the snatch on the way to winning a gold medal in the 56 kilogram division. He finished ahead of two lifters from China, silver medalist Liu Shoubin and bronze medalist Luo Jianming. Bulgaria's Ivan Ivanov equaled the Olympic record in clean-and-jerk in the 52 kilogram weight class to secure a title. China's Lin Qisheng won the silver medal and Romania's Traian Ioachim Ciharean captured the bronze.

India, traditionally strong in this event, loses to Germany in field hockey.

Silver goes to the Italians.

Silver medal to Lin Qisheng from China for the under-52-km category.

Ivan Ivanov from Bulgaria lifts 265kg to win the gold medal.

Page 64-65
Australian Kieren Perkins in the 200m freestyle.

DAY

A Chinese diver dominated her opponents to win gold, while a comeback swimmer celebrated; a Japanese volleyball victory is decided away from the court; Magic Johnson is hobbled but USA's basketball team rolls on.

A Dream Continues without Magic

In its first match, the Croatian team is beaten by the United States 103-70.

Magic Johnson, one of the world's most celebrated sports figures, saw his Olympic ambitions sidetracked by injury in a 103-70 basketball victory by the USA team over Croatia.

Johnson limped off the court early in the first half with a strained muscle in his right knee, but the absence of the prime point guard made little difference. Croatia was considered the strongest threat to the USA juggernaut in this Olympic tournament, yet such a threat never materialized.

"This team could play without a lot of people," Johnson said, refusing to be discouraged.

Although Croatia's team featured six members of the former Yugoslavian powerhouse that won the 1988 Olympic silver medal – including Toni Kukoc, Drzen Petrovic and Stojko Vrankovic – it was no match for the USA's basketball

sqnad. Kukoc is considered the hottest player in Europe, but USA's Scottie Pippen concluded in post-game remarks that Kukoc is "not as great as people said."

As comeback stories go, the one authored by U.S. swimmer Pablo Morales will rank among the best in Olympic swimming history. Morales, a multiple medalist at the 1984 Games in Los Angeles, won the men's 100-meter butterfly and the second USA swimming gold medal in Barcelona to complete his determined re-emergence at the age of 27.

Morales had been denied the 100 butterfly title in 1984 and appeared poised for another try four years later. But that bid never came about. In the USA Trials of 1988, Morales failed to qualify for the team and soon retired from the sport to pursue a law degree. Then, in 1991, Morales struggled with the death of his mother and soon yielded to a strange yearning to return to the pool. In Barcelona his comeback reached a dramatic climax, as he won "his" event in 53.32 seconds, fractions ahead of Polands Rafal Szukala (53.34). Surinames Anthony Nesty was the bronze medalist.

"Winning the gold medal is a dream come true," Morales would say.

The International Volleyball Federation (FIVB) acknowledged a referee's error and reversed the outcome of a USA-Japan men's volleyball match that had been played less than 24 hours before. Japan was awarded a 3-1 victory, nullifying the original 3-2 triumph by the two-time defending Olympic champions from the United States.

FIVB ruled that Japan should have been credited with a penalty point in the fourth game of the match, which eventually was won by the USA. Middle blocker Bob Samuelson was assessed his second yellow card of the match in the pivotal fourth game, but the infraction was never recorded on the scoresheet and Samuelson said he was not informed that the violation had been called against him. Under FIVB regulations, Samuelson's second yellow card should have translated into a penalty point for Japan.

"The team as a whole is extremely disappointed," said U.S. team captain Scott Fortune. "To battle for three hours and come out victorious, only to have people off the court decide the outcome on the court, is disheartening."

In diving, China continued to flex it's muscles in the women's platform final. Defending world champion Fu Mingxia captured the gold medal, outscoring silver medalist Elena Mirochina of the Unified Team by nearly 50 points, 461.43 to 411.63. Mary Ellen Clark of the United States won the platform bronze.

"Fu has set a new standard for women's diving," said Ron O'Brien, the veteran U.S. diving coach. "She has set a new level in terms of degree of difficulty similar to what (Greg) Louganis did in 1983."

Clark, who at 22 was considered slightly ancient by diving's typical standards, vowed that she would not remain competitive for another Olympic cycle: "This is my first Olympics and last."

Pablo Morales gets the gold in the 100m butterfly, beating Rafal Suzkaia from Poland and Anthony Nesty from Surinam.

Victory for the Unified Team in women's pistol shooting, thanks to Logvinenko's outstanding performance.

Pages 70-71
Mingxla Fu, 13, becomes the
youngest gold-medalist in the
Games.

Anita Nall, bronze-medallist,
hugs the Japanese girl Iwasaki
Kyoko, who has just beaten
the Olympic record for 200m
breast-stroke.

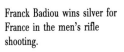

Franck Badiou wins silver for France in the men's rifle shooting.

After winning bronze in the 100m freestyle, Franziska Van Almsick gets the silver in the 200m freestyle.

DAY

Led by powerful performances the Unified Team emerges
with a gold medal in women's gymnastics; two stars of
1988 from the U.S. swimming team encounter
disappointment; the Pocket Hercules triumphs yet again.

GYMNASTICS DRAMA

The American great, Matt Biondi, is defeated; he finishes only 6th in the 100m freestyle.

Names, flags and politics may change ever more rapidly, but sport can provide stability and a link to former identity. This was vividly demonstrated on the final night of women's team competition in gymnastics. Now a collection of independent republics, but still anchored by the talents of the old Soviet Union sports machine, the Unified Team defiantly claimed the gold medal on the shoulders of 1988 Olympian Svetlana Boguinskaia.

The former world all-around champion, Boguinskaia put together a typically solid performance, allowing the former Soviet team to hold off Romania and the United States. The margin of victory was tight: 395.666 (Unified Team), 395.079 (Romania); and 394.704 (United States).

It was a particularly crucial evening for reigning world champion Kim Zmeskal of the U.S., whose individual point contribution to her team's total left her 12th overall, but more importantly, in the top three among her teammates. That meant advancement to the all-around phase of competition, where the sport's new stars are coronated.

In the aftermath of a tense session of competition, famed U.S. coach Bela Karolyi, a Romanian defector, suggested without much doubt that he would consider retirement from coaching following the Games in Barcelona. Some were skeptical, believing the master of motivation was merely attempting to give his gymnasts a psychological

boost by urging them to go out and win one last time for the "old man."

Zmeskal was in jeopardy of missing the cut for the all-around because she was 32nd individually going into the last night of the team phase. But a score of 9.95 on her final vault raised Zmeskal's total to 39.687, the best of the evening.

For the U.S., it was a banner night. The nation had not won a women's gymnastics medal in the Olympics since 1984.

As swimming's grueling week of tension continued, Germany's Dagmar Hase pulled off a mini-upset in the women's 400-meter freestyle event, winning the gold medal with a time of 4:07.18. This was at the expense of defending 400-meter Olympic champion Janet Evans of the U.S., who tearfully settled for the silver.

"I think I died a little at the end," Evans would say.

Nicole Haislett, captain of the American quartet, sets the world record for the 4×100m freestyle.

Janet Evans, from the USA, after winning gold in the 800m freestyle in Seoul does it again in Barcelona.

Similarily, in the men's 100-meter freestyle, the once invincible Matt Biondi of the U.S. ran out of steam and finished fifth. The man who won five gold medals at the 1988 Games in Seoul was left shaking his head in disbelief.

Although far removed from Biondi's world record (48.42), the Unified Team's Alexandre Popov emerged with the freestyle gold medal with a clocking of 49.02 seconds.

Weightlifting produced a stirring victory this day by the already legendary Naim Suleymanoglu, a Bulgarian expatriate who competes for Turkey. He became only the 11th weightlifter in history to collect a second Olympic gold medal, winning the 60 kilogram class with a total lift tally of 320 kilograms. Known inside the sport as the "Pocket Hercules," a name owed to the incredible strength he summons from a compact body, Suleymanoglu fell short of equalling the world record he established at the 1988 Olympics, yet his total was a healthy 15 kilograms ahead of silver medalist Nikolai Peshalov, his former Bulgarian countryman.

China scored another weightlifting medal with He Yingqiang's bronze in the 60 kilogram class.

French Open tennis champion Jim Courier of the U.S. won his first match of the Olympic tournament, suggesting later that he did not view his Barcelona assignment as any less strenuous or important than the major tennis tournaments he competes in around the world.

"This feels like a Grand Slam (event) to me," Courier would say after beating India's Ramesh Krishnan in four sets. "I'm taking it very seriously."

The International Olympic Committee created a minor controversy, stepping in to demand more details amid charges that two Olympians were practicing part-time journalism during the Games. The two are, naturally, high-profile names – track superstar Carl Lewis and basketball's Charles Barkley, both of the United States.

Although IOC Charter rule No. 59 states clearly that no credentialed Olympic athletes is permitted to "act as a

journalist" during the Games, the IOC has relaxed the bye-law in a number of cases, saying that individuals can contribute their thoughts and emotions to diaries for hometown newspapers.

But Lewis and Barkley were appearing in mass-circulation publications, Lewis in El Periodico de Catalanya, a newspaper, as well as L'Equipe magazine, Barkley in the nationally published newspaper USA Today. After being briefed by the U.S. Olympic Committee, the IOC declared the matter settled. Since both were lending their names to "columns" that are based on interviews with other journalists, rather than actually writing the material, the IOC agreed to let Lewis and Barkley continue.

"I will definitely abide by the rules of the IOC," Lewis would say.

Stevens from Great Britain wins against Salgado from Cuba: a victory which gave him the silver medal.

Page 78-79
Naim Suleymanoglu lifts the
equivalent of five times his
weight: 320Kg!

Lori Strong from the
Canadian gymnastic team.

The American team placed
third in the gymnastics.
Shown here, Kim Zmeskal.

Leos Hlavacek, TCH. Mollet
shooting range.

Shannon Miller in action at
the Palau Sant Jordi.

DAY

*A proud gymnastics tradition comes to a victorious end;
diving's Mark Lenzi fulfills a dream; the world record for
swimming's 400-meter freestyle is established anew.*

THE LAST STAND

After five difficult competitions, Poland's Skrzypaszek wins the modern pentathlon.

Page 84
Li Xiaoshuang wins the silver medal in gymnastics for China.

It was a night for savoring old memories, but also a night made bittersweet by its tone of finality. It was the night Leonid Archaev and his gymnasts made their last stand, and a triumphant one at that.

Inspired by the performances of five current or past world champions, the gymnasts of the former Soviet Union, competing in Barcelona as members of the Unified Team, rolled to the men's team title and to the top of the gold medal podium at Palau Sant Jordi arena. It was a repeat of the Soviet victory in 1988 and marked the fifth time since 1972 that a Soviet men's team — or, in this case, a team comprised of gymnasts from the former union — has finished either first or second in the team competition.

China won the silver medal, trailed by the bronze medalists from Japan.

Archaev, who has coached world-class gymnasts in Moscow for the past 20 years, did not dispute the unpleasant fact that any celebration of his team's victory would be tempered by knowledge that an era had ended. Starting with the 1996 Games, the former Soviet republics will assemble separate teams.

"I expect gymnastics to fall for a short while," said Archaev, refering to the quality of teams from the individual republics.

As an added insult, the Unified Team is not permitted to raise a flag other than the Olympic flag when its members win medals. The old Soviet anthem, heard so often at past Olympiads, has been replaced by the Olympic anthem.

"It was a flag dear to all our hearts," Archaev was saying. "I do experience some sadness, some dissatisfaction that we are not competing under the flag of our country."

Archaev then announced that he would leave Russia "to move abroad and to coach abroad."

The day's diving competiton saw Mark Lenzi of the United States win a gold medal in the men's springboard event, while China's Tan Liangde settled for his third consecutive silver medal. Tan was second in the 1984 and 1988 Games to legendary diver Greg Louganis, who ironically was the inspiration behind Lenzi's decision to become a diver himself.

"I don't know what happens, but I am never at my best in the finals," Tan said. "Mark Lenzi performed incredibly well."

Lenzi moved into first place after the seventh of 11 dives and proceeded to widen his margin with increasing degrees of difficulty on every subsequent dive. Tan clung firmly to second place, while Dmitri Saoutine of the Unified Team fought his way to the bronze medal.

An emotional Bill Lenzi, father of the gold medalist, explained that he was not supportive of his son's decision in 1986 to switch from wrestling to diving. In reflection, he said his son obviously was wise to follow his heart.

"I was trying to direct him toward being a wrestler," Bill Lenzi said in the emotional aftermath of Mark's victory. "He said, "No, diving." We had a falling out. But he proved me wrong and I guess sometimes parents don't always know what is best for their kids."

As with gymnastics, the Unified Team proved to be a dominant presence in the swimming pool, where Evgeni Sadovyi set a world record in the 400-meter freestyle for men. He was clocked in 3 minutes, 45 seconds and secured his third gold medal of the Games.

Sadovyi's fellow swimmer Elena Roudkovskaia surged to a gold medal in the women's 100-meter breaststroke race with a time of 1:08, finishing ahead of 16-year-old Anita Nall of the United States. A fifth swimming medal was collected by China when Hong Qian established an Olympic record of 58.62 to win the 100-meter women's butterfly event, and, once again, the result raised questions about China's rapid improvement in women's swimming.

The central question was linked to rumors that Chinese swimmers are the benefactors of performance-enhancing drugs. But Qian was defiant in her response to charges.

"There are (drug) tests," she would say. "If there was dopage, the results would come out. We've never used dopage."

Japan scored a major women's volleyball victory, defeating the United States in five sets in an opening-round game. Later, the Japanese coach, Kazunori Yoneda, described the triumph as a miracle.

Other gold medalists on Day 5 included judo's Odalis Reve Jimenez of Cuba, in the middleweight division; three Unified Team competitors in Greco-Roman wrestling (Alexandr Karelyn, 130 kilograms; Oleg Kucherenko, 48 kilograms; Mnatsakan Iskandarian, 74 kilograms); and Lee Eun Chulwon of South Korea in shooting's free rifle/prone event.

Iran's Ali Kazemi, a boxer, was eliminated from the Games on a bitter note, victimized by a transportation mixup that seems to occur with amazing regularity at the Olympics. Kazemi, like the 1988 U.S. Olympic boxer Anthony Hembrick, missed his bus to the boxing venue, arriving late for his bout with Pakistan's Asghar Muhammad. It was an innocent mistake, but the Iranian was disqualified.

200 m breaststroke: Mike Barrowman swims for the highest podium.

With his third gold medal, Sadovyi becomes the swimming king.

Neiwand (AUS), Magne (FRA) and Chiappa (ITA) on the Horta velodrome.

Jozef Tracz (POL) gets
Olympic gold in the under
74kg greco-roman wrestling
competition. The picture
shows the match between
Almanza (CUB) and Kornbakk
(SWE).

Great Britain's Kate Howey wins the judo bronze medal in the under 66kg class.

Swimming: a day of records.

Page 93
The Mexican Jorge
Mondragon earns loth place
in diving. The event was won
by the American Lenzi.

Page 90-91
The first gold medal for the
British team won by Chris
Boardman.

DAY

6

Olympic and world swimming records take a pounding as Chinese swimmers grow in stature; the newest queen of gymnastics almost misses the ball; drug testing's dark cloud visits the British team.

CHINA BUILDS BARCELONA LEGACY

"Tarzan" Nelson Diebel wins the gold medal.

Page 94
Trillini from Italy defeats china's Huifeng Wang in fencing.

Alexander Popov, here with Matt Biondi, become the world's fastest swimmer by winning the 100m and the 50m competitions.

Summer Sanders going for the silver medal in 200m individual medley.

The victory of Li Lin makes the seventh gold medal for China. Li Lin broke the oldest world swimoning record.

World records continued to be eclipsed at the Olympic swimming pool, including the longest standing mark for the 200-meter individual medley. That standard was surpassed by yet another emerging star from the People's Republic of China, 21-year-old Lin Li, who completed the event in 2 minutes, 11.65 seconds, erasing the record set 11 years earlier by Ute Geweniger of the former German Democratic Republic (East Germany).

It was China's sixth swimming medal of the Games, quite an improvement by a swimming program that garnered zero medals at the 1984 Olympics and four at the 1988 Games in Seoul.

Meanwhile, the Unified Team punctuated its domination of the men's swimming sprints with Alexandr Popov's victory in the 50-meter freestyle. The Unified Team won

all of the sprint events as the steady decline of short-distance specialists from the United States – Matt Biondi and Tom Jaeger – became evident once again. Until Barcelona, the U.S. had not been shut out of the gold medals in the 100, 200 and 400 freestyle events since 1960. And in the 50, added to the Games four years ago, the drought continued, with Biondi finishing second and Jaeger third.

But Biondi has collected a total of 10 Olympic medals since 1984 and that, he would say after the defeat, is still worth something.

"When I read the newspaper, I look at 10 Olympic medals, and I've got a smile from ear to ear," he said.

The day was sweeter for several other prominent American swimmers, however, as Melvin Stewart wiped away memories, still lingering after four years, of a haunting loss to Germany's Michael Gross in the 200-meter butterfly. Janet Evans made history by repeating as champion of the 800 freestyle, and the U.S. 400-meter medley relay team crushed the world record.

Stewart, a comedian no doubt in another life but a very talented swimmer in this life, established an Olympic record in the 200 "fly", completing the distance in 1:56.26 – an improvement of .68 seconds on Gross' former mark.

Evans, a double gold medalist in 1988, overcame a disappointing earlier loss in the 400 to capture the 800 in

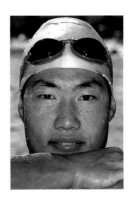

Li Lin breaks the world record in 200m individual medley.

A srelte Svetlana Boguinskaia is not able to match her performance in Seoul.

For Gutsu, her sudden coronation marked a rapid turn of fortunes. She had been the fourth-rated Unified Team gymnast following the team competition and, thus, was not supposed to have qualified for the all-around phase. However, when teammate Roza Galiyeva pulled out because of a knee injury, Gutsu took her place and clearly made the most of the opportunity. The raising of the flag of Ukraine, a former republic of the dissolved Soviet Union, in recognition of Gutsu's gold medal is believed to be an Olympic first.

Miller, the more fragile looking of the American duo that she formed with Zmeskal, was praised later by her coach as having managed "the greatest achievement by anyone (from the U.S.) since Mary Lou Retton," the 1984 Olympic champion.

The flag of Moldova also made its debut at the Summer Games when it was raised to recognize the gold medal earned in weightlifting by Fedor Kassapou, a member of the Unified Team. Kassapou's total in the middleweight division (75 kilograms) was 357.7, and although it was matched by Cuban Pablo Lara Rodriguez, Kassapou scored the title because he entered the day with a lower body weight than Rodriguez.

An annoucement that has become almost expected at the Games dampened the spirits of the British Olympics team, Just one day before the start of track and field, the British delegation announced that sprinter Jason Livingstone, indoor world recordholder at 60 meters, was sent home following results of a drug test showing the presence of a banned anabolic steroid. The test had been taken two weeks earlier, prior to Livingstone's departure for Barcelona. Additionally, British officials said weightlifters Andrew Davies and Andrew Saxton also had proven positive in preliminary tests and were banished from the Games as well.

8:25.52. Her world record (8:16.22) was never challenged, but Evans was relieved, saying, "I've been through a lot in the last four years (and) it made winning even more sweet.

If there's been a (challenge), I could have gone faster. But does it matter?"

The newest darling of women's gymnastics came to the fore on Day 6 in the all-around, the results of which provided a clear reminder that the generations come and go like a blur in gymnastics. The dominant figures less than one year earlier at the 1991 world championships — American Kim Zmeskal and Svetlana Boguinskaia of the Unified Team — were pushed aside by the pixie-like Tatyana Gutsu (Unified Team), Shannon Miller (U.S.) and Lavinia Milosovici (Romania). Boguinskaia finished fifth, Zmeskal an incredible 10th.

Page 100-101
Germanys Sabine Bau
concentrating before the
confrontation.

The table tennis competitions
take place in the North
Stadium.

Windsurfers training in the
Olympic harbor. Great Britain
is the favorite.

DAY

7

The "new" Ben Johnson gets back on track; Shcherbo
leads the way in a Unified Team sweep of the men's
gymnastics all-around medals; an Australian swimming
star smashes his world record.

BEN JOHNSON RETURNS

Jon Ronningen full of joy after his victory in greco-roman wrestling.

A big disappointment for the Swiss champion Werner Günthör who could not repeat his victory at the world championships in Tokyo.

Olympic cyclists making their rounds.

Four years after a positive drug test tainted track and field, the Olympic Games, and his own reputation, Jamaican-born sprinter Ben Johnson returned to the starting blocks to pursue a new chapter in his career.

Competing again for Canada, Johnson advanced through two heats and into the semifinals of the men's 100 meters event with unusual fanfare, given the reality that he was only an average competitor and no longer the world's fastest human being.

Though still swift, Johnson could not run away from the memory of the Seoul Games, where he set a world record of 9.79 seconds and defeated American Carl Lewis in the marquee showdown of the meet - only to be shamed by a drug test that revealed the presence of an anabolic steroid.

After completing his heats, the first in 10.55 and the second in 10.30, Johnson, no longer the imposing physical specimen who once appeared invincible, sounded very

much like a man delighted by a second chance in the Olympic spotlight.

"I'm not feeling any pressure right now," he would say. "I'm just happy to be here."

The opening day of track and field competition featured the surprising gold-medal performance of American competitor Mike Stulce, who became the first U.S. shot putter to win the Olympic title since 1968. Stulce had not been a prominent face in the event because of a two-year suspension for a positive drug test that ended in the months leading to the Barcelona Games. Stulce captured the gold with an effort of 21.70 meters, trailed by silver medalist and fellow American team member James Doehring (20.96). The Unified Team's Viatcheslav Lykho claimed the bronze medal with a distance of 20.94 meters.

Unlike Canada's Johnson, the comeback of South Africa's Zola Budd Pieterse ended as quickly as it started. Remembered by track fans for her collision with American

Mary Decker in the 1984 Games of Los Angeles when Budd represented Great Britain, she finished ninth in her first-round heat in the 3,000 meters and failed to advance in Barcelona.

Next door to the Olympic Stadium, at Palau Sant Jordi arena, the men's gymnasts of the Unified Team continued to dominate, this time in the all-around phase of competition. The medals sweep was led by Vitaly Shcherbo, 20, a citizen of the republic of Belarus. Grigori Misutin of Ukraine took the silver medal, followed by bronze medalist Valeri Belenky of Azerbaijan.

Afterwards, Shcherbo reflected with a tone of sadness on the inevitable breakup of the once-powerful gymnastics factory formed under the now-vanished umbrella of the Soviet Union's elite sports system. He was especially quick to mention the important role of Leonid Archaev, the former Soviet and current Unified Team coach.

"He really is the best in the world," Shcherbo would say.

The Olympic swimming pool hosted its final events of the 1992 Games on Day 7, and the finale was marked by the shattering of numerous world records, not to mention Matt Biondi's emergence as one of the most prolific medal winners in history.

Biondi, the U.S. star in the twilight of his career, shared in America's gold medal finish in the 4×100 men's medley relay by swimming in a qualifying heat. It was the 11th Olympic medal Biondi has collected since 1984, thus allowing him to tie Mark Spitz and shooter Carl Osburn for the U.S. record for total career medals.

Other world-record performances were put forth by Australia's Kieren Perkins, the USA's Jeff Rouse and China's Yang Wengyi. Perkins swam a time of 14 minutes, 43.48 seconds in the 1,500-meter freestyle, improving his world record by 4.92 seconds. Rouse, competing in the medley relay, set the world standard for the 100-meter backstroke and helped the U.S. match the world-best time of 3:36.93. China's Yang finished the 50 freestyle in 24.79

seconds, bettering her world record of four years ago. Her teammate, Zhuang Yong won the silver medal in the 50.

A showdown in men's basketball between the Unified Team and Lithuania did not produce the storybook ending some had predicted, as the Unified Team overcame a 19-point lead by Lithuania to win 92-80. The game featured former teammates recast as opponents, owed to Lithuania's complete break from the old Soviet Union and the recognition of its autonomous Olympic committee. Four years ago in Seoul, the Soviet team won the gold medal with a lineup that included four current Lithuanian and four Unified Team members.

The victory, led by Valeri Tikhonenko's 31 points, allowed the Unified Team to clinch first place in its pool with a 4-0 record. Lithuania suffered its first Olympic tournament loss after three wins despite being considered a favorite in the contest. A month earlier, Lithuania had defeated the Unified Team by 37 points in an Olympic qualifying game. Sarunas Marciulionis, who plays in the National Basketball Association with the Golden State Warriors, scored 21 points for his native Lithuania.

The track and field competition began with a victory by a Catalan athlete in the 20km walk. Local favorite Daniel Plaza was greeted in the Olympic stadium with a standing ovation by 60,000 spectators.

Valeri Belenki wins bronze
behind her teammates
Chtcherbo and Misoutine.

Li Xiaosahuang finishes 5th in
gymnastics, a competition that
was dominated by the athletes
of the Unified Team.

A jubilant Pyrros Dimas after lifting 370Kg for Olympic gold.

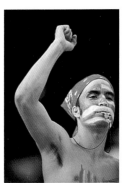

The canoe and kayak training
started today in Castelldefels.
Pictured are the Americans
Scott and Jacobi.

Jean-Paul Adam from Senegal
failed to qualify for the finals
of the 200m medley.

DAY

Speed reigns at the Montjuïc Olympic Stadium, where the
fastest humans have their finest hours; a gold medal
favorite is upset by a Spanish opponent in boxing and
controversy rages; tennis underdogs prosper.

Gail Force on Montjuic

The fastest man in Barcelona on Aug. 1, 1992, was 32-year-old Linford Christie, a native Jamaican competing for Great Britain in the Olympic 100 meters. He ran the distance in 9.96 seconds, later calling the performance "the best race of my life." Christie was certain of that, he would say later, with 40 meters yet to be run. "They said I am an old man," said Christie, who is in fact the oldest winner of the 100 meters in Olympic history. "At about 60 meters, I knew I had it won."

There was to be no showdown similar to the Ben Johnson-Carl Lewis affair of four years ago when Johnson won in a world-record time that was later nullified when he tested positive for an anabolic steroid. But Christie was nonetheless impressive, outsprinting silver medalist Frank Fredericks of Namibia, a nation being represented in the Games for the first time, and Dennis Mitchell of the United States, the bronze medalist.

While Christie's emergence in what was thought to be the twilight of a 12-year career was stirring, his counterpart on the women's 100 gold medal podium, American Gail Devers, authored the final chapter of an even more incredible story on Day 8.

Perhaps any talented sprinter considers herself blessed with great speed, yet Devers arrived at the 1992 Games just thankful that she still had the ability to put one foot in front of the other. She won the 100 in 10.82 seconds, a fraction ahead of Jamaicas Juliet Cuthbert and four others in an extremely close finish that required a photo examination. But the miracle of Gail Devers was not that she won the Olympic title, it was that she recovered so thoroughly, and in less than two years, from a nearly crippling and mysterious illness.

"Last year I couldn't walk," said Devers, who was not exaggerating. In 1991, doctors finally diagnosed an overlooked condition known as Graves Disease. The radiation treatments that followed were incorrectly administered, causing the malfunction of her thyroid, and Devers escaped the necessity of amputation with only days to spare. Her feet blistered and "hurt so much I had to crawl."

The grueling women's marathon, run on a typically sweltering Barcelona day, left the two top finishers overcome by exertion, although it quickly turned to relief. That relief became joy for the Unified Team's Valentina Yegorova,

---

Page 112
The world's fastest humans embark on a ten second quest.

Dana Chladak (USA) struggles for control in the canoeing slalom final.

Jockeying for position.

Linford Christie of Great Britain, the oldest 100m champion in Olympic history, celebrates his upset victory.

the winner in 2 hours, 32 minutes, 41 seconds. She held off Japans Yuko Arimori over the last three miles.

World champion boxer Eric Griffin of the United States was brought to his knees in the Olympic boxing hall by a fundamental flaw in the new electronic scoring system adopted, ironically enough, to eliminate inequitable judging. Griffin, a heavy favorite to win the Olympic title at 106 pounds, lost a 6-5 decision to Spain's Rafael Lozano, which prompted shock waves of disbelief. Analysis of blows registered by both boxers by the five-judge panel later revealed that Griffin had been credited with 81 landed punches to only 50 for Lozano.

The electronic system registers a point each time three of the five judges acknowledge the same punch within one second. Given Griffins status as a four-time world champion, the decision was immediately appealed to the a review board of the International Amateur Boxing Association.

"They stole the fight from me," Griffin would say, devastation in his voice. "I'm sure I scored 25 to 30 points. ... This was the worst decision I ever got. They had something set up when I stepped into the ring."

Lozano, as was to be expected, viewed the scoring and his victory in dramatically different terms.

"This is the most important win of my sporting career," he said. "(Griffin) threw more punches than I did, but mine were more penetrating and more effective and so I scored more points."

The outcome was eerily reminiscent of the 1988 Olympic tournament in which American boxer Roy Jones was eliminated by a decision in favor of a South Korean opponent, who later acknowledged that he was beaten.

In tennis, the Games bid farewell to their top mens players, American Jim Courier and Germany's Boris Becker. Courier was defeated in a third-round match in straight sets by Switzerland's Marc Rosset, while Becker exited after a four-set defeat to Fabrice Santoro of France.

Rosset was as surprised as the spectators by Courier's demise, saying that his primary Olympic objective had been "to be with the other athletes and see the other sports."

Romania's Lavinia Corina Milosovici won two of the four apparatus finals in women's gymnastics, capturing gold medals in floor exercise and vault. Later, Romanian coach Octavian Bellu proclaimed his countrys program, modeled after the old Soviet Union, ready to move to the top of the sport.

"We have the potential to be the leaders," he said.

Meanwhile, frustration had taken its toll on famed gymnastics coach Bela Karolyi by the conclusion of the womens competition. His prime Olympic title hopeful, Kim Zmeskal, collapsed in the all-around and continued to struggle in the event finals. She was upstaged by U.S. teammate Shannon Miller, who won a silver in the balance beam and bronze medals in uneven bars and floor exercise.

Cuba's Dulce Garcia reaches
for his best.

No medal for Canada's Ben
Johnson.

Shooting the rapids in the K1 slalom final.

A spectator contemplates his own brand of shooting at the rifle range.

Australians are victorious in double skulls.

Birgit Clarius of Germany prepares to give it her best shot during the first day of heptathlon competition.

Page 121
America's Gail Devers, a surprise winner in the 100m with a time of 10.82 seconds.

DAY

An established star, Joyner-Kersee rises again in the heptathlon; the world's No. 3 men's tennis player falls to an underdog; gymnast Shcherbo places his final stamp on an unforgettable Olympic performance.

EYES ON TRACK AND FIELD

S ustained excellence, the ultimate goal of any world-class athlete, is Jackie Joyner-Kersee's signature on the Olympic heptathlon. The American who overcame poverty in childhood to attain stardom became the gold medalist and undisputed world's greatest female athlete for the second time in four years in Barcelona.

Never before had anyone repeated as the Olympic heptathlon champion, and Joyner-Kersee discovered just how difficult the task really is. Not only had she struggled the day before in the shot put — recording her worst effort in two years — but she also had to contend with a challenger, Germany's Sabine Braun, who made several attempts to intimidate Joyner-Kersee as the competition unfolded.

Prior to one Joyner-Kersee long jump attempt, Braun managed to brushagainst her, walking past at a blatantly inopportune moment. This merely inspired the American, as it turned out, and Braun's strategy eventually backfired altogether. The 1991 world heptathlon champion finished third behind Irina Belova of the Unified Team.

"Everytime they do that, that's going to cost them the Olympic championship," said Bob Kersee, Jackie's husband and coach, refering to Braun's tactics. "They can charge her all they want and she'll hold the red cape up in their face and won't blink."

The only flawed aspect of Joyner-Kersee's title was that her winning total (7,044) fell short of the heptathlon world record she set at the 1988 Seoul Games. But it was more than sufficient to secure the gold and to outdistance Belova (6,845) and Braun (6,649).

In the final strides of the final event, the 800 meters, Joyner-Kersee knew the title she had been unable to pursue at the 1991 world championships because of a pulled hamstring was hers. "It was a feeling of relief and joy when I crossed that line," she said later.

I. Astaprovich takes the silver in the hammer. Teammates A. Abduvaliyev (gold) and I. Nikulin (bronze) completed the sweep for the Unified Team.

Page 122
S. Amegatcher of Ghana is injured in a 400m qualifying run.

The 1500m wheelchair was a demonstration event.

Italian gold medal winner P. Ferrazzi during kayaking (K-1) finals.

Water polo competitors fight for posession. Australia beat France 9-5 in this preliminary match.

6-3 victory against No. 3-ranked Pete Sampras of the United States. Of the top eight seeds in the men's field, only Croatia's Gordon Ivanisevic, the 1992 Wimbledon runnerup, remained alive.

Cherkasov was humble in victory, saying it was "unbelievable."

Another Unified Team Olympian, this one subject to much greater expectation than his tennis playing fellow teammate, thoroughly dominated the final evening of men's gymnastics competition. Vitali Shcherbo won four apparatus gold medals, raising his gold total to six. He had collected the first in the team event and the second in securing the coveted all-around individual title.

Shcherbo's triumphs in the apparatus final came in parallel bars, pommel horse, rings and vault. He tied Pae Gil Su of North Korea for the parallel bars gold, as Pae became his country's first Olympic gold medalist since 1976.

Boxing remained the focus of controversy as the debate surrounding four-time world champion Eric Griffin's loss at 106 pounds was formally closed by the sport's international federation. Griffin's appeal, submitted by USA Boxing, of a 6-5 loss to Spain's Rafael Lozano was rejected by the International Amateur Boxing Association even though the written scorecards of a jury monitoring the bout would have made Griffin the winner.

Another major highlight of Day 9 was provided by Javier Sotomayor, who emerged as Cuba's first track and field medalist since 1980. Although he did not threaten his world record (8 feet), established in 1989, Sotomayor completed all of his jumps without a miss and captured the gold with a leap of 7 feet, 8 inches. Sweden's Patrik Sjoberg also recorded a 7-8 jump, but received the silver because of an earlier miss. Three high jumpers tied for the bronze medal, all at the same 7-8 height, but with misses along the way.

Upsets continued to mount at the Olympic tennis stadium, where the Unified Team's Andrei Cherkasov, the world's 26th-ranked male player, scored a 6-7 (7-9), 1-6, 7-5, 6-0,

Javier Sotomayor of Cuba won the gold medal in the high jump with a jump of 2.34 meters, well below his world record. Three other competitors also cleared the same height, but the Cuban was awarded the gold on the basis of fewer misses.

The official scoring was generated by an electronic system that requires at least three judges to register a point within one second. Despite being viewed as an innovation, the system still relies on the reaction time of the judges seated before the control panel. U.S. coach Joe Byrd compared its potential flaws as being similar to a typewriter operated by someone who does not know how to type.

In men's basketball, Croatia, Lithuania, Brazil and Venezuela were winners on the final day of preliminary games. Croatia was guaranteed a spot in the upcoming quarterfinals phase, so it allowed many of its key players to rest on the bench. That decision nearly resulted in a loss to Angola, which led by 18 points before succumbing to Croatia's 32-5 scoring run in the game's closing minutes.

The day's surprise note was delivered by Italy, which won its first road cycling title at the Olympics in 24 years.

Page 127
America's Patrick Ewing towers over his Spanish opponent.

Jackie Joyner-Kersee leaps for long jump points in the heptathlon. The American defended her Olympic title with a total of 7044 points.

Page 128-129
The rowing events were dominated by the Canadians and the Germans.

Birgit Clarius selects her javelin for the heptathlon competition. The German eventually finished 7th.

Page 132-133
China's Li Jing is caught in top form.

DAY 10

Holland's Van Langen proves superior in the 800; an eight-year journey ends for a Canadian hurdler; Mike Conley triple jumps into history; Spain controls the seas.

TRIUMPH, REDEMPTION AND RECORDS

Page 134
The team dressage competition ended with an equestrian victory for the Germans.

The finish of the 10,000m resulted in controversy.

Ellen Van Langen showed patience and a final burst of desire to set herself apart from a talented field in the women's 800 meters, winning the gold medal by a narrow margin and fulfilling the expectations of her countrymen.

"Many in Holland expected me to win the gold because I had the world's fastest time this year," Van Langen said after recording a time of 1 minute, 55.54 seconds. "There were eight girls, all very fast. Luckily, I was the one."

The Unified Team's Lilia Nurutdinova mounted a serious threat in the final 100 meters, but could not catch the winner and was left with the silver medal after a clocking of 1:55.99. Meanwhile, one of Cuba's premier track stars of recent years, Anna Quirot, made her Olympic debut successful by winning the 800 bronze in 1:56.80. She had struggled through a difficult year, the low point of which had been the death of her coach.

"I've had only five 800-meter races in 1992, due to injury," Quirot would say later. "Of course, I was thinking about getting a gold medal. But the bronze medal is tantamount to gold in my case because I was deprived of an Olympic opportunity before this year."

Before a sun-drenched crowd that peaked at 65,525 during the afternoon session at Barcelona's Montjuic Olympic Stadium, Canada's Mark McCoy gained redemption, the USA's Mike Conley grabbed an Olympic record, and China's Yueling Chen walked into Olympic history.

In the men's 110-meter hurdles, McCoy sought to end the disappointment he had known in two previous Olympic appearances, the first in 1984 when he was fourth in the event. He left little doubt that he was ready this time, winning the gold medal with the second-fastest time in Summer Game's history (13.12 seconds), thus becoming the oldest 110-meter hurdles champion (31) to enter the Olympic record book.

The moment was especially gratifying given McCoy's bitter memory of the 1988 Games in Seoul, where he finished seventh in the hurdles final. Disappointed, he returned home early without the authorization of Canadian officials and was ultimately suspended.

"After 1988, I seriously considered quitting," said McCoy. "I never believed I'd be sitting here today (with a gold medal). I'm not sure if this makes up for 1988, but I've forgotten about the whole thing. It was a bad episode."

Conley, the 1984 Olympic triple jump silver medalist, proved he's only getting better at age 29, as he established the Olympic record in the event with a leap of 18.17 meters. His only regret after winning the gold medal was that the distance was wind-aided and not registered as a world record.

The veteran Canadian Mark McKoy takes just 13.12 seconds to win the gold in the 110m hurdles, finishing ahead of Tony Dees and Jack Pierce of the United States.

Ellen Van Langen wins gold for Holland as she crosses the finish line in the 800m final.

"But asking for anything more (than a gold) is just being greedy," said Conley, who had not qualified for the 1988 Seoul Games.

China once again demonstrated its growing status as a world sports power when Chen collected her country's first track gold medal, winning the 10 kilometer walk race.

The Cuban men's volleyball team, on a mission to reach a gold-medal final against the talented U.S. squad, easily rolled past South Korea on Day 10 in a rematch of a previous World Cup showdown.

"Personally, I thought it would be closer," Cuba's Raul Diago said. "When we played Korea a few months ago, they were a much more competitive team."

The women's volleyball tournament also featured a strong Cuban presence. Cuba completed the preliminary phase atop its bracket and automatically qualified for the semifinals, as did the Unified Team in the other bracket.

With its mastery of the yachting competition, Spanish pride was in full force on the Barcelona waterfront, where gold medals were collected in the Flying Dutchman and Finn division to give Spain four golds and one silver at these Summer Games. France also proved dominant, as Frank David won the Olympic title in the men's Lechner class and Yves Loday in the Tornado class.

American Mike Conley triple jumps to Olympic gold.

"With this gold," declared David, "I may have proved that the new generation of [French] yachtsmen can equal or even replace the old greats."

For the first time in Games history, no U.S. woman was present on the medals podium after the women's springboard diving final. The gold medalist was another of China's precisionists, Gao Min, while the top U.S. finisher was fifth-place Julie Ovenhouse.

"It just didn't happen," said Ovenhouse. "But not very many people can say that they are Olympians, and that's something that no one can take away from me."

Perhaps no one demonstrated the spirit of being an Olympian this day better than Great Britain's Derek Redmond, who pulled a hamstring during his 400 meters semifinal race and was rendered virtually immobile. Instead of quitting, however, Redmond limped to the finish, drawing the applause of a huge track and field crowd that recognized his plight.

Waiting for Redmond at the end of his nightmarish journey was his father, Jim, who had gotten past barriers around the track to greet his hobbled son.

"I just wanted to finish," Derek Redmond would say later. "It was as simple as that."

Ronny Weller of Germany
took the gold in the 110Kg
class.

Page 140-141
The Chinese are spectacular in the diving events: Min Gao spins gold on the springboard.

Concentration at the archery range.

Page 143
Jamaica's Ottey and Cuthbert embrace after the 100m final.

DAY

First a Moroccan, then a Kenyan stake claim to the
10,000 meters gold, but the original winner prevails in a
round of appeals; China sweeps up new titles in diving
and table tennis, but loses a volleyball player to a drug
ban; Cuba eyes a medals harvest in boxing.

PROTESTS AND SLUGFESTS

The longest 10,000 meters battle perhaps ever contested at the Summer Olympics reached a conclusion on Day 11. It developed into a bizarre case of "who's got the gold?" and was finally resolved after a whirlwind of appeals and counter-appeals.

Khalid Skah of Morocco was the presumed winner of the event the day before when he crossed the finish ahead of Kenya's Richard Chelimo, but the Kenyan delegation immediately filed protest, arguing that Skah's teammate, Hammou Boutayeb, had intentionally hampered Chelimo to assist Skah.

Boutayeb was running with the other two in the final laps, but was actually a lap behind the frontrunners when the jostling began. The first appeal by Kenya led to Skah's disqualification and made Chelimo the Olympic champion.

But less than 24 hours later, the International Amateur Athletic Federation (IAAF) reversed the ruling after reviewing a counter-appeal by the Moroccans.

Thus, Skah was reinstated as the gold medalist and a subsequent Kenyan appeal of the new ruling was dismissed.

Skah, who had won the first time in 27 minutes, 46.7 seconds, claimed from the start that he had pleaded with his teammate, Boutayeb, to "go away" and leave the two leaders alone.

There was similar bickering at the weightlifting venue, but this was a war of words between members of the same delegation. Residents of different republics, lifter Alexander Kourlovitch of Belarus, and former Olympic champion Vassili Alexeyev of Russia, apparently do not see eye to eye on how to build a world-class program.

After winning the gold medal in the super heavyweight class and claiming the title of world's strongest man, Kourlovitch lashed out at Alexeyev, who has risen to become head of Unified Team's weightlifting federation – a federation that was scheduled to dissolve after the Games when all the former republics of the Soviet Union go their separate ways.

"There are people who act like dictators, and this is the simplest way to characterize Mr. Alexeyev," said Kourlovitch, who claimed his gold with a combined lifting total of 450 kilograms. "He attempted to not include me here, but I was supported by people (ranking) above him."

Kourlovitch pointed to the exclusion of light heavyweight lifter Altymourad Orazdoudyev of the republic of Turkmenistan. He said Alexeyev simply decided to throw him off the team.

Indonesia collected a pair of gold medals – the nation's first-ever in the Olympics – courtesy of two badminton players who are coincidentally romantic companions. Susi Susanti won the women's singles title and her boyfriend Allan Budi Kusuma captured the men's singles title on the same day.

Page 144
Japan's dreams of baseball gold were dashed by Chinese Taipei 9-5.

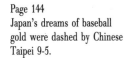

Even Olympic mascot Coobi sports Ray-Bans.

Platform diver Michael Kuhne against the blue Barcelona sky. The German finished 7th. China's Sun Shuwei captured the gold.

146

Meanwhile, China struck another gold medal blow in table tennis, as Lu Lin and Wang Tao captured the men's doubles event, defeating a German doubles team 26-24, 18-21, 21-18, 13-21, 21-14. But it was not an altogether victorious day for the Chinese delegation, which was informed that a member of its women's volleyball team tested positive for a banned substance.

The International Olympic Committee announced that Wu Dan's urine samples revealed the presence of the stimulant strychnine and that the player would be banned from a seventh-place game against Spain. The chairman of the IOC's medical commission, Prince Alexandre de Merode of Belgium, said the player reported having consumed a "tonic" containing capsules she had brought along from China. Wu characterized the capsules as a popular "folk medicine."

Cuba continued to excel in its favorite sports — baseball and boxing. The Cuban boxing team advanced nine athletes into the semifinals, which means they are guaranteed at least bronze medals in each of those weightclasses. One of the victims of Cuba's assault was U.S. super heavyweight Larry Donald, who was dominated by reigning world amateur champion Robert Balado in a quarterfinal bout.

Donald was believed to be suffering from the lingering effects of a ligament injury to his right hand, but he did not mention that after Balado scored a 10-4 decision.

"He won the fight," Donald said. "I just had a bad day."

And the U.S. team apparently is just having a bad tournament. Through the quarterfinal phase, it was assured of only three medals — the lowest U.S. total in Olympic boxing since 1956.

In baseball, Cuba recorded a 6-1 semifinal victory against the USA and set up a gold-medal encounter with Taiwan.

A 16-year-old whisp of a diver named Sun Shuwei walked away with the men's platform title on Day 11 — China's third diving gold medal of the Games. Sun punctuated the performance on his final dive, a 3 1/2-

Host team Spain edges Korea 2-1 in the field hockey semifinal.

Equestrian Simon Hugo jumping for Austria. The Austrians finished second to the Netherlands in the team final.

A French crew catches the wind during a Soling class match. In the final standings, the boat manned by Spain's Prince Felipe finished 6th.

Action around the field
hockey goal.

Page 148-149
A furious start at
Castelldefels, site of the
canoeing and kayaking events.

somersault tuck, by earning perfect scores of "10" from four members of a seven-judge panel.

"Great quickness," said the USA's Scott Donie, who won the platform silver. "The Chinese spin so fast that they create a greater margin of error — and you only get that with lots of repetition.

As the Games gradually reached a conclusion, more and more athletes found themselves finished with competition and with plenty of time to celebrate. But officials at the athletes' village along Barcelona's waterfront decided that too much of a good thing was becoming a problem for other residents who still needed to sleep at night. They announced that the village restaurant would close between the hours of 1 a.m. and 6 a.m. In Barcelona, however, moving the party to another location would not prove too difficult.

Page 151
Sugiara wheels and deals...

Ernesto Aguero of Cuba
prepares to snatch 230Kgs.

Before each lift, Aduche Ojadi
gulps for strength-giving air.
The Nigerian finished tied for
last.

DAY

12

Another drug scandal clouds the Games; records established in the men's 200 and 400, while heralded Michael Johnson runs out of steam; an era of U.S. invincibility in women's basketball ends.

WATTS LIGHTS UP THE TRACK

Jud Logan's fourth-place finish in the hammer throw event was surprising. But the subsequent revelation that he had failed a drug test was shocking.

Word of Logan's pending dismissal from the Summer Games spread rapidly on Day 12, and was followed by an another International Olympic Committee announcement that marathoner Madina Biktagirova had tested positive for a banned stimulant. Like Logan, the Unified Team member had not won a medal in the Games, finishing fourth in the marathon.

Later that same evening, IOC Medical Commission chairman Prince Alexandre de Merode confirmed that Logan, a five-time U.S. hammer throw champion, turned up positive for Clenbuterol, a stimulant with properties similar to anabolic steroids which can increase human muscle mass.

The drug is often prescribed to treat asthma, but Medical Commission member Arnold Beckett said, "It is accurate to say it is used for other purposes."

De Merode's admission was considered unusual because Logan's testing procedure technically was not completed at the time of verification.

Away from the laboratory and on the track, Olympic records were shattered in two men's events — the 200 and 400 meters. American Quincy Watts claimed the 400 gold medal after running the second fastest time in history (43.50 seconds) and surpassing the record of 43.71 he had established in the semifinals.

The 200 semifinals provided moments of greatness and despair. Mike Marsh of the United States was the one basking in the glory, setting an Olympic record of 19.73 seconds. "I think it's possible to set a world record in the final," Marsh promised.

No world records would be in store for the heralded U.S. 200-meters star Michael Johnson, who exited the Games in the semifinals, failing to advance despite running against what most experts considered lesser opponents. He was sixth in the semifinals.

"In the home stretch, I just didn't feel like Michael Johnson," he would say. "It just wasn't there."

Johnson's problem might not have been so mysterious, however. An undisclosed illness, he said, had sapped some of the energy he was accustomed to having in reserve for a major meet. "In the back of my mind, I was very afraid the sickness had taken some of my strength."

Upset victories of major proportions transpired in women's basketball and men's volleyball on Day 12. Riding an incredible 15-game winning streak in the Olympic Games, the U.S. women's basketball team was viewed as being almost as much of a nightmare for opponents as the men's Dream Team. But dreams of victory came true for the Unified Team, as it engineered a stunning 79-73 upset that left the U.S. with a bronze medal as its highest ambition. Unable to defend its 1984 and 1988 Olympic titles, team members were devastated, especially because some had played on those previous gold-medal squads.

"This will leave a scar for the rest of our lives," said U.S. player Teresa Weatherspoon.

The Unified Team coach, Eugeni Gomelsky, savored the victory and questioned the USA's style of play: "Their tactics are no good, in my opinion."

Marie-José Pérec wins the 400m gold for France.

Page 154
Japan defeats USA 8-3 to win the bronze medal in baseball. Cuba won the gold and Chinese Taipei captured the silver. Will we see an American Dream Team - baseball-style - in 1996?

In volleyball, the stunner of the day was delivered by the Netherlands, which eliminated defending world champion Italy in the quarterfinal round. "We prepared especially for Italy," said Dutch coach Arie Selinger.

Cuba, absent from the Summer Olympics since 1980, continued to be a force in Barcelona. Its legendary baseball team rolled to the gold medal, toppling Taiwan 11-1, while Japan collected the bronze medal by defeating the United States 8-3.

Spain's hopes for a medal in women's tennis faded away, as the United States' Jennifer Capriati dispatched Arantxa Sanchez-Vicario in three sets, thus securing a gold medal showdown with Germany's Steffi Graf. The Vicario-Capriati match was witnessed by King Juan Carlos of Spain and his family, but Capriati quickly showed why she is royalty in the sport of tennis, winning the first set 6-3. She stumbled in the second, allowing Vicario to make a mild comeback but rebounded in the third set.

Graf easily advanced to the final with a straight sets win against Mary Joe Fernandez of the U.S., 6-4, 6-2. It was over in just 69 minutes.

Romania's Costel Grasu
finished 4th in the discus.
Romas Ubartas won the gold
medal for Lithuiania.

Preliminary competition in the 100m hurdles.

Dave Johnson (USA) clears the bar during the first day of the decathlon competition.

Quincy Watts set a new Olympic record in the 400m, covering the distance in 43.50 seconds.

Page 160-161
The powerful stride of premier French sprinter Marie-José Pérec.

Johnson at the finish of the decathlon 100m dash. He was in 9th position after the first five events.

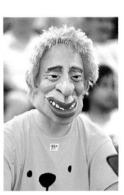

DAY

13

On a day of triumph for U.S. track stars, the ever-present
Lewis steals the show with his third long jump title;
Kevin Young obliterates the 400-meter hurdles world
record; the decathlon title belongs to Zmelik.

KING CARL

arl Lewis rose and rose and kept rising to the occasion, in this case the Olympic long jump final. And when it was over, his legendary status in track and field had been lifted yet another notch as Lewis, 31 years young, won his third consecutive Olympic gold medal in the event with a leap of 28 feet, 5 1/2 inches.

Most of the suspense was in the waiting because Lewis' winning jump was recorded on his first attempt, which created a target of sorts for the likes of Mike Powell, the event's world recordholder, and Joe Greene, U.S. teammate of both Lewis and Powell.

"I felt it would be a gauge for everyone to shoot for," Lewis would say.

So into the night they pressed on, taking their best shot at the mark. But the mark would not fall. It held up throughout, with Powell managing a silver-medal jump of 28-4 1/4 on his final attempt, and Greene coming in third with a best jump that was a foot shy of Powell's best.

"He's the best ever," said Powell, whose problems with a hamstring hindered any possibility of matching his 1991 world record (29-4 1/2). "A lot of things are said on and away from the track, but I have a tremendous amount of respect for Carl. He's the best jumper of all-time."

Lewis, who did not qualify for the 100 meters at these Games, arrived in Barcelona without the usual fanfare. He would not have a chance to reclaim the title of world's fastest man, and he only was named to the U.S. relay team after Mark Witherspoon was injured. And the long jump? Well, that was Powell's event, wasn't it? Yet in just a few seconds time, Lewis had secured his seventh Olympic gold medal dating to 1984.

As always, he was crowned King Carl for another night.

Earlier on Day 13, the decathlon battle was decided and Kevin Young of the United States pulled off a stunner in the men's 400-meter hurdles.

With co-favorite Dave Johnson of the U.S. plagued by an ankle stress fracture, the decathlon opened up to all serious challengers, and it was Robert Zmelik of the Czech and Slovak Federative Republic (formerly Czechoslovakia) who seized the opportunity.

Zmelik amassed 8,611 points, using a strong performance in the 110-meter hurdles to gain momentum in the day's opening decathlon event. Spain's Antonio Penalver won the silver medal, staying in the thick with an 864-point discus toss, and Johnson struggled from ninth entering the final session to claim the bronze medal.

Page 164
Gwen Torrence (USA) and Grace Jackson (JAM) embrace after the 200m final. Torrence won the gold while Jackson finished 6th in the event.

I can't believe it! Paraskevi Patoulidou realizes she has just won the 100m hurdles. The little-known Greek sprinter won the event after Gail Devers of the US tripped over the last hurdle.

Johnson was held back in the pole vault and passed on a final attempt that might have added to his 8,309 total.

"It just hurt too much," the former world decathlon champion said, refering to the troublesome ankle. "If everything had been healthy, we'd be talking about (a gold medal) right now."

That's precisely what hurdler Young was talking about after setting the world record — crushing the old mark — with a time of 46.78 seconds. The clocking slashed .24 off the existing mark established in 1983 by Edwin Moses.

"I didn't think I'd see the day in my generation that somebody would bust (Moses') world record," said Kriss Akabusi of Great Britain, the bronze medalist.

Young called the performance "my little niche in history," the first sub-47 second 400 hurdles ever run coming as it did amid the spotlight of the Olympic Games.

All in all, the U.S. left a major stamp on the day's track events, winning six golds, three silvers, and a pair of bronze medals. A seventh gold medal was one hurdle away from being in the books, but Gail Devers tripped over it, lost her lead in the 100-meter hurdles and settled for fifth. This allowed an obscure runner from Greece, Paraskevi Patoulidou to claim the gold medal.

North Korea picked up another freestyle wrestling gold medal in a showdown with its neighbor to the south. The 48-kilogram title went to North Korea's Kim Il, who defeated South Korean Kim Jong Shin 4-1. Another South Korean, Park Jang Sun was more fortunate, winning the 74-kilogram title 1-0 against Kenny Monday of the United States, the 1988 Olympic gold medalist. Monday's loss was particularly disappointing because the only point he yielded throughout the entire Barcelona tournament ultimately cost him a repeat gold.

Gatien of France won silver in the table tennis singles.

Kerry Shacklock of Great Britain takes her turn in the synchronized swimming competition.

The men's 200m final. America's Mike Marsh won in 20.01, Frank Fredericks of Namibia finished 2nd, and Michael Bates of the US took the bronze.

Leading up to this point, America's Gail Devers falls over the last hurdle in the 100m final. She got up to finish 5th.

Page 169
Pelota, a sport popular in Spain, is a demonstration event in Barcelona.

In men's tennis, where underdogs dominated from the start, the last seed in the tournament was eliminated by Marc Rosset of Switzerland. He defeated Croatia's Goran Ivanisevic 6-3, 7-5, 6-2, and advanced to the gold-medal final, where Rosset will face Jordi Arrese of Spain who ousted the Unified Team's Andrei Cherkasov in the other semifinal.

Ivanisevic found consolation in his bronze medal, knowing that any degree of success in the Olympics would be embraced as a victory by countrymen in his troubled homeland.

"You can't know how it feels," the Croat would say. "When I play Wimbledon, it's for myself. Here, it is for my country."

World record holder Mike Powell could not stop Carl Lewis from winning his third consecutive Olympic long jump title.
Powell won the silver.

Page 172, 173
The finish of the 110m
decathlon hurdles.

Carl Lewis leads American
jumpers to a 1-2-3 sweep in
the long jump.

DAY

14

Champion pole vaulter Bubka falters and fails to medal;
Germany's Drechsler triumphs in the long jump, while
Olympic teammate Graf is upset by a U.S. teenager in
the tennis final; Cuba rises in women's volleyball.

THE RISE AND FALL OF BUBKA

Maybe it was the swirling wind, maybe not. Or maybe it was never meant to be. But whatever the mysterious force was, it sufficiently foiled the world's premier pole vaulter and sent him away from the Olympic Games without a medal of any color.

Sergei Bubka, Olympic and world champion, world recordholder and athletic god, made three attempts, two at the same height, and missed them all on Day 14. And without pausing to explain his unexpected demise, he was gone. Just like that. No medals, no records, no glory.

The Ukraine legend issued only a brief statement, suggesting he was the victim of "my nerves playing up on me."

"Most of us," Bubka said, "had problems with the swirling wind around the field and the run-up (to the bar), and I was definitely one of them."

Still some were not as troubled by the conditions. The gold was claimed by another member of Bubka's Unified Team. Clearing a height of 5.80 meters, Maxim Tarassov edged teammate Igor Trandenkov, who cleared the same height but required three attempts. The bronze went to Spain's Javier Garcia Chico, who needed only two tries to make 5.75 meters — the mark Bubka missed on his third and final attempt — thus denying American Kory Tarpenning the third spot. Tarpenning attained 5.75 on his third leap.

"I've got one weeping eye and one smiling one," Trandenkov would say. "My very good friend and teacher, Sergei Bubka, didn't achieve what he wanted, but his pupil took the silver."

A similarly unexpected development involving a world-class star unfolded in the women's long jump, as defending Olympic champion Jackie Joyner-Kersee of the United States fell short of her optimum effort and had to settle for a bronze medal. Although she had repeated as Olympic heptathlon champion earlier in the Games, Joyner-Kersee expressed disappointment after her best jump of the afternoon measured only 7.07 meters.

"I've jumped in conditions with the wind in my face before," she would say later. "That's no excuse. This is the Olympics — you give it your best shot."

Benefiting from the champion's misfortune was Germany's Heike Drechsler, who won the long jump gold medal with a leap of 7.14 meters, edging the Unified Team's silver medalist Inessa Kravets. The outcome was especially rewarding for the German jumper because it marked the first time in her career that she had demonstrated superiority over Joyner-Kersee. At the 1988 Games in Seoul, Drechsler was second, and the same scenario repeated itself at the world championships last year in Tokyo.

Before the day was through at the Olympic Stadium on Montjuic, a moment of historical significance would emerge in the women's 10,000 meters. First to the finish was

Page 174
Mexico's Carlos Mercenario, silver medalist in the 50km walk, competes against the Barcelona heat as well as the other athletes.

The failure of world recordholder Sergei Bubka to win a medal in the pole vault is a shocker. But teammates Tarassov and Trandenkov of the Unified Team picked up the slack by winning gold and silver.

Tim Bright (USA) descends from an unsuccessful vault.

Drive, she said. But the Unified Team drove to the gold.

"May I introduce you to the mat!"

Ethiopia's Derartu Tulu, followed by a white South African named Elana Meyer, who became the first from her politically isolated nation since 1960 to win an Olympic track and field medal.

Meyer had long been considered one of the world's top female distance runners, but a ban on international sports participation had denied Meyer and her South African teammates the opportunity to showcase their talents on the world stage. In Barcelona, South Africa returned to the Olympic Games for the first time in 32 years and Meyer responded to the once unthinkable opportunity.

"It was amazing," Meyer would say, "to get on the track and know this is for the whole of South Africa — and for the real South Africa."

After the race, Meyer and Tulu, who is black, joined hands and trotted around the stadium track to celebrate a victory that was both about sport and the struggle for racial unity.

Women's tennis witnessed the crowning of an unlikely Olympic champion in 16-year-old American Jennifer Capriati, who defeated defending singles gold medalist Steffi Graf of Germany, the world's No. 2-ranked female. Capriati, winless against Graf in four previous career attempts, overcame a 3-6 deficit after the first set to polish off her foe 6-3, 6-4.

Cuba ascended to the top of the world in women's volleyball, capturing the gold medal with a four-set victory against the Unified Team. In the former days of the Soviet

Union, the Unified Team squad had been a dominant force, winning four Olympic titles. But this time it settled for a silver medal, followed by the bronze medalists from the United States, who defeated Brazil.

Brazil's men fared much better, defeating the U.S. juggernaut volleyball team to advance to the gold-medal game. The U.S. team had won the last two Olympic titles.

Poetry in motion: Penny and Vicky Vilagos of Canada win the silver in synchronized swimming.

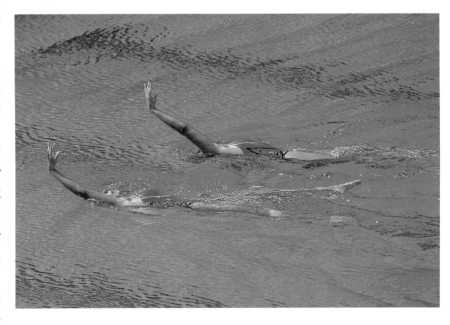

An impressive medal sweep
for Kenya in the 3000m
steeplechase.

Spain wins the gold by defeating Germany 2-1 in field hockey.

Cuba dominates the boxing competition.

Elana Meyer of South Africa after finishing 2nd in the 10,000m. Later she would run a victory lap with gold medal winner Derartu Tulu of Ethiopia.

Page 183
Heptathlon winner Jackie Joyner-Kersee also won a bronze in the long jump.

Page 180-181
16-year old American Jennifer Capriati upset gold medal favorite Steffi Graf of Germany in the singles final.

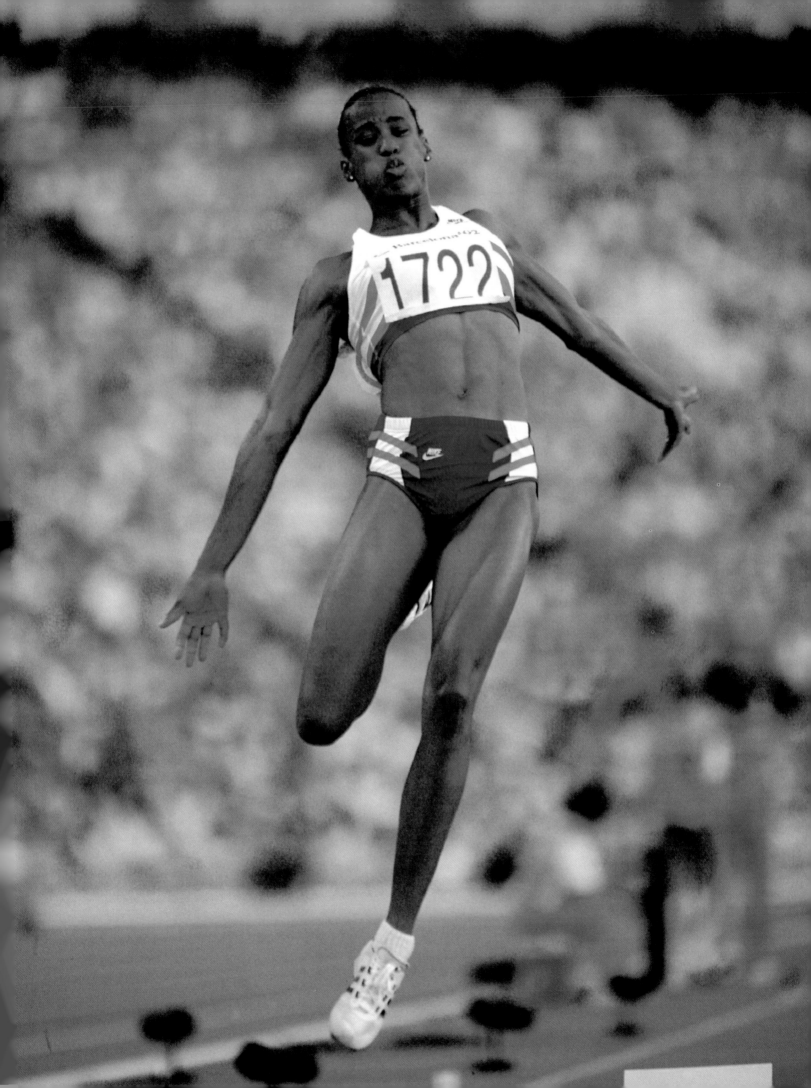

DAY

15

A basketball team enhances its legend by realizing a
golden dream; U.S. relay teams are record-setters; Spain's
sweetest Olympic moment is also its most dramatic; Cuba
reaps a harvest of gold in the ring.

DREAMERS

Page 184
Awaiting another attack...

A Nigerian boxer contemplates a new strategy between rounds.

Gold medal winner Savon of Cuba batters an opponent during heavyweight final bout.

The Unified Team found the handle on the gold medal in team handball.

Nigerians celebrate a medal winning performance in the 4×100m relay.

roatia brought a determined and talented men's basketball team to the 1992 Summer Games, and its appearance in the gold-medal title game was especially important to a country struggling for independence. Indeed, this was a team of heroes just for having assembled and played in Barcelona.

But it was not supposed to be a team flirting with the impossible, leading the invincible United States men's squad 25-23 at the midway point of the first half. And it was never expected to be so pesky as to be trailing the heavily favored Dream Team by a relatively close margin (56-42) at the intermission.

So even after the USA professional stars pulled away to claim the title that would never be denied, not in anyone's wildest imagination, Croatia had placed its stamp on the Olympic tournament. The Croats emerged as the Dream Team's most unwilling victim, losing by only 32 points, 117-85. It was the narrowest margin of victory for the U.S. during the Games.

This, of course, did not make the decisive victory anything less than sweet for the Americans.

"We were able to do what everyone expected us to do," Michael Jordan would say after scoring 22 points.

The expected began to take shape in the second half when the U.S. outscored Croatia 11-2 and gained a 67-44 advantage with less than 18 minutes remaining. Later, the celebration began, as the Dream Team was introduced for the long awaited medal ceremony, flanked by the silver medalist Croats and the bronze medalists from Lithuania.

"This was a majestic team," said the U.S. coach Chuck Daly, the normally high-profile figure who was largely a spectator during the Games.

Charles Barkley, the outspoken member of the group who spiced the tournament with his verbal arrows aimed at the U.S. Olympic Committee, was visibly mellowed by the experience of having a medal draped around his neck. He had been criticized for mocking the USOC, but on this night Barkely cast that aside and savored the moment.

He promised his medal would be presented to the high school where he once was a student in Leeds, Alabama. This is "to let them know that a fat little black kid from a small southern town could make it somewhere in life," Barkley said.

On the final night of track events before the Aug. 9 men's marathon, two relay teams would heat up the running surface of the Montjuic Olympic Stadium. Both set world records. Both were teams from the United States.

Leading the way in the 400-meter relay was none other than Carl Lewis, who matched former Olympian Ray Ewry by picking up his eighth career gold medal. Lewis arrived at the Games without the expectation of running the relay, but Mark Witherspoon's injury created a vacancy and Lewis stepped in. As if to punctuate what he had already achieved — a third straight title in the Olympic long jump — Lewis anchored a world record effort, finishing off what Mike Marsh, Leroy Burrell and Dennis Mitchell had started. The clock read 37.40, as the U.S. outdistanced Nigeria and Cuba.

"After the worst month of my life competitively, I could never imagine the Olympics ending with two gold medals and a world record," said Lewis, who failed to qualify for the the U.S. in the 100 meters. "It's incredible."

Also incredible is that Lewis has been part of the four fastest 400 relays in track history.

Matching the 100-meter team for thrills was the 1,600-meter foursome of Andrew Valmon, Quincy Watts, Michael Johnson and Steve Lewis, which set a world record of 2:55.74, blitzing the runners-up from Cuba and the bronze medalists of Great Britain.

The triumph was especially important to Johnson, who had been eliminated from the men's 200 in the semifinals and denied a chance to contend for the gold medal many believed he was destined to win.

A crowd of 95,000 witnessed Spain's brush with disaster in the Olympic soccer final, a disaster that was averted when, in the game's final minute, Francisco Narvaez slipped a shot past Polish goalkeeper Alexander Klak to secure a 3-2 victory.

Spanish treasure: Fermin Cacho of Spain crosses the finish line to win the 1.500m.

"Internationally speaking, this is the greatest feat as far as a Spanish team is concerned," Spanish coach Vicente Miera would say.

For the host country, it marked the first Spanish soccer medal since the 1920 Games in Antwerp.

Spain also advanced to the water polo final, defeating the U.S. men 6-4, while Fermin Cacho scored another triumph for his Spanish countrymen by winning the gold medal in the 1,500 meters.

Cuba's Ariel Hernandez, scoring a 12-7 decision against the USA's Chris Byrd, was one of four boxers from that country to collect golds on Day 15.

Picture perfect: Carolina Pascual of Spain demonstrates perfect form in rythmic gymnastics. She brought home a silver in the event.

Page 188-189
The Netherlands vs. powerhouse Pakistan in field hockey action.

Page 192-193
The Unified Team's Timoshenko on her way to gold in rhythmic gymnastics.

Page 191
Marc Rosset wins the only medal of the games for Switzerland, a surprise gold in men's singles.

A world record smile for Carl Lewis.

Page 194
The golden dream is fulfilled: Final score, United States 117 - Croatia 85.

Spain scores in the last minute of play against Poland to break a 2-2 tie and win the soccer gold.

Page 192-193
Polish gymnast Joana Bodak bends over backwards to impress the judges.

DAY

16

Conquering the grueling final stages, South Korea's Hwang wins the marathon; Cuba realizes its boxing destiny with three more gold medals; Brazil is king of men's volleyball, marking a new era; the Games conclude and the world turns its eyes to Atlanta and 1996.

FAREWELL AND ON TO ATLANTA

After 16 days, a marathon of Olympic activity marked its conclusion with a personal marathon of triumph for South Korea's Hwang Young-Cho, who ran in solitude through the final phase of the men's course, up the grueling incline to Montjuic and into a cheering throng inside the Olympic Stadium.

More than 65,000 spectators watched as Hwang easily won the race in 2 hours, 13 minutes, 23 seconds, nearly half a stadium lap ahead of Japan's Koichi Morishita, the silver medalist, and Germany's Stephan Timo Freigang, winner of the bronze. In the final, triumphant strides, Hwang raised his weary arms and his smile reflected the joy of an entire city, the joy that swells from within when the job is done and done well.

The moment was especially poignant for the South Korean.

"The last time a Korean won the marathon (56 years prior to the very day), it was done under the Japanese flag," he said. "I was happy and moved to have done it today under the Korean flag."

It had been a tense battle with Morishita, but Hwang pressed on and finally passed his foe at about the 35-kilometer mark.

"When I entered the stadium, I was fairly sure, but not absolutely certain. In the Olympics, you can lose at the last minute. And then I saw my whole life passing in front of me at the medals ceremony."

Morishita conceded that his opponent had something extra: "I tried not to lose my concentration, but Hwang ran strongly at the end."

On the final day of boxing, the ever dominant Cubans picked up three more gold medals and departed Barcelona with a total of seven boxing titles. The winners on Day 16 were light welterweight Hector Vinent, light middleweight Juan Lemus, and super heavyweight Robert Balado. North Korea collected a gold in the flyweight division, won by Choi Chol, while Germany earned a light heavyweight title courtesy of Torsten May.

The men's volleyball medals also were decided in the final hours of the Games, with Brazil capturing the gold medal against The Netherlands, and the United States winning the bronze-medal game over Cuba.

"The hardest thing for the Dutch team was stopping our attack from all positions," said Antonio Gouveia, the Brazilian coach. "These Games have seen a significant change: The eternal champions are no longer so dominant."

"The standard of play in volleyball has improved throughout the world, and there is greater equality between teams than before."

Gouveia credited his team's emergence to the "spirit between the players and our coaches."

After the marathon finishers had passed the final wire, the Olympic Stadium buzzed with anticipation and the closing ceremony of the XXVth Olympiad was soon underway. On a crystal clear evening in Barcelona, spectators and a global television audience witnessed an intense display of pageantry, dancing, and music.

Then it was left to dignitaries Pasqual Maragall, the mayor of Barcelona and head of the local organizing

Page 196
The moon is a balloon!

The marathon capped the track and field competition on the final day. Hwang of Korea finished first in the classic distance with a time of 2:13.23.

Brazil defeated the Netherlands in the volleyball final. The favored USA team came away with a bronze.

Ludger Beerbaum takes equestrian gold for Germany.

Flamenco is featured in the closing ceremony.

committee, and Juan Antonio Samaranch, president of the International Olympic Committee, to close the Games. Samaranch praised Barcelona, the region of Catalonia, and the nation of Spain for its excellent execution of the event, then participated in the symbolic passing of the Olympic flag, in this case from Barcelona to the waiting grasp of Atlanta and its mayor, Maynard Jackson.

In four years, the Centennial Olympic Games will belong to the city of Atlanta, to the state of Georgia and to all the United States.

"Mayor Jackson defined the Atlanta Games as the Games of the future in a city of the future, and I think that is a very good point," Maragall would say. "Every four years, there is room for improvement.

"I have recommended to the mayor of Atlanta that they should organize their own (unique) Games because that is part of the fun of it."

The celebration climaxed with the arrival of the Games' athletes, who flooded onto the stadium surface and created a sea of spontaneous colors. There was laughter and dancing and happiness. If only for a moment, the world was suspended in time and mankind was at peace.

The closing ceremony is
underway.

The sky lights up over the
National Palace.

Man still struggles against the elements.

A Spanish bull seems delighted with the festivities.

Fireworks illuminate Montjuïc.

Page 204-205
The Barcelona Games, soon to be a fond memory.

BARCELONA'92 SUMMER GAMES IN FACTS AND FIGURES

THE PROGRAM

The Olympic Program included 28 sports:
Archery
Athletics (Track and Field)
Badminton
Baseball
Basketball
Boxing
Canoeing
Cycling
Diving
Equestrian
Fencing
Football
Gymnastics
Handball
Hockey
Judo
Modern Pentathlon
Rowing
Shooting
Swimming
Synchronized Swimming
Table Tennis
Tennis
Volleyball
Water Polo
Weightlifting
Wrestling
Yachting

And two demonstration sports:
Pelota
Taekwondo
A total of 812 medals were awarded over 16 days of competition. During the Games, athletes set 28 new world records and 86 Olympic records in six sports.

PARTICIPANTS

A record number of 172 national teams were represented and a total of 10,253 athletes (7,330 men and 2,923 women) participated in the games. The USA was the largest contingent with 1,049 members (609 athletes), while the smallest was the Solomon Islands with three members and one athlete.

Aside from athletes, there were 4,845 team officials plus an additional 1,966 extra team officials for a total of 17,064 sports participants.

Over the eight days of athletic competition, 752,705 spectators attented the Olympic Stadium.

COMMUNICATIONS

The Barcelona Olympics featured a private information network called AMIC (Multiple Access to Information and Communication). The network consisted of 2,000 terminals, 600 printers, and 1,700 software programs. Over the course of the 16-day Olympiad, the system facilitated:

6,500 biographies of athletes plus 400 other personalities

Up to 450,000 consultations per day

2 million printed pages

1.8 million result information queries

1.5 million news and general queries

1.4 million electronic mail messages by 62,000 users

129,184 total users

More than 8 million total queries

MEDIA COVERAGE

4,102 print journalists and 778 photographers were accredited from 1,700 media organizations. International radio and TV correspondents accounted for an additional 11,434 journalists for a total of 16,314 media representatives.

Including observers, volunteers, suppliers, and guests, a grand total of 129,184 people were accredited by the Olympic Organizing Committee.

Accredited photographers took over 3,156,000 photos.

2,750,000 photocopies were distributed to the press.

While working, members of the press consumed 21,250 litres of drinks, including 10,000 litres of water, 3,600 litres of beer, and 12,000 cups of coffee.

MEDALS TABLE

COUNTRY	GOLD	SILVER	BRONZE	TOTAL
Unified Team	45	38	29	112
United States of America	37	34	37	108
Germany	33	21	28	82
People's Republic of China	16	22	16	54
Cuba	14	6	11	31
Spain	13	7	2	22
Korea	12	5	12	29
Hungary	11	12	7	30
France	8	5	16	29
Australia	7	9	11	27
Italy	6	5	8	19
Canada	6	5	7	18
Great Britain	5	3	12	20
Romania	4	6	8	18
Czech and Slovak Fed. Republic	4	2	1	7
D.P.R. of Korea	4	0	5	9
Japan	3	8	11	22
Bulgaria	3	7	6	16
Poland	3	6	10	19
Netherlands	2	6	7	15
Kenya	2	4	2	8
Norway	2	4	1	7
Turkey	2	2	2	6
Indonesia	2	2	1	5
Brazil	2	1	0	3
Greece	2	0	0	2
Sweden	1	7	4	12
New Zealand	1	4	5	10
Finland	1	2	2	5
Denmark	1	1	4	6
Morocco	1	1	1	3
Ireland	1	1	0	2
Ethiopia	1	0	2	3
Algeria	1	0	1	2
Estonia	1	0	1	2
Lithuania	1	0	1	2
Switzerland	1	0	0	1
Jamaica	0	3	1	4
Nigeria	0	3	1	4
Latvia	0	2	1	3
Austria	0	2	0	2
Namibia	0	2	0	2
South Africa	0	2	0	2
Belgium	0	1	2	3
Croatia	0	1	2	3
Indep. olympic participant	0	1	2	3
Islamic Republic of Iran	0	1	2	3
Israel	0	1	1	2
Chinese Taipei	0	1	0	1
Mexico	0	1	0	1
Peru	0	1	0	1
Mongolia	0	0	2	2
Slovenia	0	0	2	2
Argentina	0	0	1	1
Bahamas	0	0	1	1
Colombia	0	0	1	1
Ghana	0	0	1	1
Malaysia	0	0	1	1
Pakistan	0	0	1	1
Philippines	0	0	1	1
Puerto Rico	0	0	1	1
Qatar	0	0	1	1
Surinam	0	0	1	1
Thailand	0	0	1	1
Total:	259	258	298	815

Abreviations:
NWR: New Worled Record
NOR: New Olympic Record
EWR: Equals World Record
EOR: Equals Olympic Record

Barcelona'92

YACHTING

MEN FINN
1.VAN DER PLOEG GARCIA, JOSE M.	ESP	
2.LEDBETTER, BRIAN	USA	
3.MONK, CRAIG JOHN	NZL	

OPEN STAR
1. REYNOLDS, MARK J. HAENEL, HAL H.	USA	
2. DAVIS, RODERICK HOPKINS COWIE, DONALD JOHN	NZL	
3. MACDONALD, D. ROSS JESPERSEN, ERIC ALBERT	CAN	

OPEN FLYING DUTCHMAN
1. DORESTE BLANCO, LUIS MANRIQUE, DOMINGO	ESP	
2. FOERSTER, PAUL BOURDOW, STEPHEN	USA	
3. BOJSEN MOLLER, JORGEN BOJSEN MOLLER, JENS	DEN	

OPEN SOLING
1. BANK, JESPER SECHER, STEEN KLAABORG SEIER, JESPER	DEN	
2. MAHANEY, KEVIN BRADY, JIM KERN, DOUG	USA	
3. SMITH, LAWRIE CRUIKSHANK, ROBERT GORDON STEWART, OSSIE	GBR	

OPEN TORNADO
1. LODAY, YVES HENARD, NICOLAS	FRA	
2. SMYTH, RANDY NOTARY, KEITH	USA	
3. BOOTH, MITCH FORBES, JOHN ROBERT	AUS	

MEN 470
1. CALAFAT ESTERLICH, JORDI SANCHEZ LUNA, FRANCISCO	ESP	
2. REESER, MORGAN BURNHAM, KEVIN	USA	
3. TONISTE, TONU TONISTE, TOOMAS	EST	

MEN LECHNER A-390
1. DAVID, FRANCK	FRA	
2. GEBHARDT, MIKE	USA	
3. KLEPPICH, LARS DETLEF	AUS	

WOMEN EUROPE
1. ANDERSEN, LINDA	NOR	
2. VIA DUFRESNE PEREÑA, NATALIA	ESP	
3. TROTMAN, JULIA	USA	

WOMEN 470
1. ZABELL LUCAS, THERESA GUERRA CABRERA, PATRICIA	ESP	
2. EGNOT, LESLIE JEAN SHEARER, JANET LEE	NZL	
3. ISLER, JENNIFER HEALY, PAMELA	USA	

WOMEN LECHNER A-390
1. KENDALL, BARBARA ANNE	NZL	
2. ZHANG, XIAODONG	CHN	
3. DE VRIES, DORIEN	NED	

GYMNASTICS

MEN COMPET. III FLOOR
1. LI, XIAOSAHUANG	CHN	9.925
2. MISIOUTINE, GRIGORI	EUN	9.787
3. IKETANI, YUKIO	JPN	9.787

MEN COMPET. III POMMEL HORSE
1. CHTCHERBO, VITALI	EUN	9.925
2. PAE, GIL-SU	PRK	9.925
3. WECKER, ANDREAS	GER	9.887

MEN COMPET. III RINGS
1. CHTCHERBO, VITALI	EUN	9.937
2. LI, JING	CHN	9.875
3. LI, XIAOSAHUANG	CHN	9.862

MEN COMPET. III VAULT
1. CHTCHERBO, VITALI	EUN	9.856
2. MISIOUTINE, GRIGORI	EUN	9.781
3. YOO, OK RYUL	KOR	9.762

MEN COMPET. III PARALLEL BARS
1. CHTCHERBO, VITALI	EUN	9.900
2. LI, JING	CHN	9.812
3. GUO, LINYAO	CHN	9.800

MEN INDIVIDUAL ALL-AROUND
1. CHTCHERBO, V.	EUN	59.025
2. MISIOUTINE, G.	EUN	58.925
3. BELENKI, VALERI	EUN	58.625

MEN TEAM C.
1. EUN	585.450
2. CHN	580.375
3. JPN	578.250

WOMEN COMPET. III FLOOR
1. MILOSOVICI, LAVINIA CORINA	ROM	10.000
2. ONODI, HENRIETTA	HUN	9.950
3. GOUTSOU, TATIANA	EUN	9.912

BOXING MEN LIGHT WELTERWEIGHT

1. VINENT CHARON, HECTOR	CUB
2. LEDUC, MARK	CAN
3. KJALL, JYRI GOERAN	FIN
3. DOROFTEI, LEONARD DORIN	ROM

BOXING MEN SUPER HEAVYWEIGHT

1. BALADO MENDEZ, ROBERTO	CUB
2. IGBINEGHU, RICHARD	NGR
3. ROUSSINOV, SVILEN ALDI-BUL NOV	
3. NIELSEN, BRIAN	DEN

BOXING MEN FEATHERWEIGHT

1. TEWS, ANDREAS	GER
2. REYES LOPEZ, FAUSTINO	ESP
3. SOLTANI, HOCINE	ALG
3. PALIANI, RAMAZI	EUN

BOXING MEN WELTERWEIGHT

1. CARRUTH, MICHAEL	IRL
2. HERNANDEZ SIERRA, JUAN	CUB
3. ACEVEDO SANTIAGO, ANI-PUR BAL	
3. CHENGLAI, ARKOM	THA

BOXING MEN LIGHTWEIGHT

1. DE LA HOYA, OSCAR	USA
2. RUDOLPH, MARCO	GER
3. HONG, SUNK SIK	KOR
3. BAYARSAIKHAN, NAMJIL	MGL

BOXING MEN BANTAMWEIGHT

1. CASAMAYOR JHONSON, JOEL	CUB
2. MCCULLOUGH, WAYNE	IRL
3. ACHIK, MOHAMED	MAR
3. LI, GWANG SIK	PRK

WOMEN COMPET. III BEAM

1. LYSSENKO, TATIANA	EUN	9.975
2. LU, LI	CHN	9.912
3. MILLER, SHANNON	USA	9.912

WOMEN COMPET. III VAULT

1. ONODI, HENRIETTA	HUN	9.925
2. MILOSOVICI, LAVINIA CORINA	ROM	9.925
3. LYSSENKO, TATIANA	EUN	9.912

WOMEN COMPET. III ASYMMETRIC BARS

1. LU, LI	CHN	10.000
2. GOUTSOU, TATIANA	EUN	9.975
3. MILLER, SHANNON	USA	9.962

WOMEN INDIVIDUAL ALL-AROUND

1. GOUTSOU, TATIANA	EUN	39.737
2. MILLER, SHANNON	USA	39.725
3. MILOSOVICI, L.	ROM	39.687

WOMEN TEAM C.

1. EUN	395.666
2. ROM	395.079
3. USA	394.704

BOXING

BOXING MEN LIGHT HEAVYWEIGHT

1. MAY, TORSTEN	GER
2. ZAOULITCHNYI, ROSTISLAV	EUN
3. BERES, ZOLTAN	HUN
3. BARTNIK, WOJCIECH	POL

BOXING MEN LIGHT MIDDLEWEIGHT

1. LEMUS GARCIA, JUAN CAR-CUB LOS	
2. DELIBAS, ORHAN	NED
3. REID, ROBIN DAVID	GBR
3. MIZSEI, GYORGY	HUN

BOXING MEN FLYWEIGHT

1. CHOI, CHOL SU	PRK
2. GONZALEZ SANCHEZ, RAUL	CUB
3. KOVACS, ISTVAN	HUN
3. AUSTIN, TIMOTHY	USA

BOXING MEN HEAVYWEIGHT

1. SAVON FABRE, FELIX	CUB
2. IZONRITEI, DAVID	NGR
3. VAN DER LIJDE, ARNOLD	NED
3. TUA, DAVID	NZL

BOXING MEN MIDDLEWEIGHT

1. HERNANDEZ ASCUY, ARIEL	CUB
2. BYRD, CHRIS C.	USA
3. JOHNSON, CHRIS	CAN
3. LEE, SEUNG BAE	KOR

BOXING MEN LIGHT FLYWEIGHT

1. MARCELO GARCIA, ROGELIO	CUB
2. BOJINOV, DANIEL PETROV	BUL
3. QUAST, JAN	GER
3. VELASCO, ROEL	PHI

HOCKEY

MEN

| 1. GER |
| 2. AUS |
| 3. PAK |

WOMEN

| 1. ESP |
| 2. GER |
| 3. GBR |

VOLLEYBALL

VOLLEYBALL MEN

1. BRA	
2. NED	
3. USA	

VOLLEYBALL WOMEN

1. CUB	
2. EUN	
3. USA	

TENNIS

TENNIS MEN DOUBLES

1. GER	
2. RSA	
3. CRO	
3. ARG	

TENNIS MEN SINGLES

1. ROSSET, MARC	SUI
2. ARRESE, JORDI	ESP
3. IVANISEVIC, GORAN	CRO

TENNIS WOMEN DOUBLES

1. USA	
2. ESP	
3. AUS	

TENNIS WOMEN SINGLES

1. CAPRIATI, JENNIFER	USA
2. GRAF, STEFFI	GER
3. FERNANDEZ, MARY JOE	USA
3. SANCHEZ-VICARIO, ARANTXA	ESP

WATER POLO

WATER POLO MEN

1. ITA	
2. ESP	
3. EUN	

EQUESTRIAN SPORTS

EQUESTRIAN SPORTS MIXED

1. BEERBAUM, LUDGER	GER	0.00
2. RAYMAKERS, PIET	NED	0.25
3. DELLO JOIO, NORMAN	USA	4.75

GYMNASTICS

GYMNASTICS WOMEN

1. TIMOSHENKO, ALEXANDRA	EUN	59.037
2. PASCUAL GRACIA, CAROLINA	ESP	58.100
3. SKALDINA, OKSANA	EUN	57.912

FOOTBALL

FOOTBALL MEN

1. ESP	
2. POL	
3. GHA	

HANDBALL

HANDBALL MEN

1. EUN	
2. SWE	
3. FRA	

HANDBALL WOMEN

1. KOR	
2. NOR	
3. EUN	

BASEBALL

BASEBALL

1. CUB	
2. TPE	
3. JPN	

FENCING

MEN SABRE TEAMS

1. KIRIENKO, GRIGORIJ CHIRCHOV, ALEXANDRE POGOSSOV, GUEORGUI GOUTTSAIT, VADIM POZDNIAKOV, STANISLAV	EUN
2. SZABO, BENCE KOVES, CSABA NEBALD, GYORGY ABAY, PETER BUJDOSO, IMRE	HUN
3. LAMOUR, JEAN-FRANÇOIS DAURELLE, JEAN-PHILIPPE DUCHEIX, FRANCK GRANGER-VEYRON, HERVE GUICHOT, PIERRE	FRA

WRESTLING

WRESTLING MEN

1. KHADARTSEV, MAKHARBEK	EUN
2. SIMSEK, KENAN	TUR
3. CAMPBELL, CHRISTOPHER L.	USA

WRESTLING MEN 82 KG

1. JACKSON, KEVIN A.	USA
2. JABRAIJLOV, ELMADI	EUN
3. KHADEM AZGHADI, RASUL	IRI

WRESTLING MEN 57 KG

1. PUERTO DIAZ, ALEJANDRO	CUB
2. SMAL, SERGUEI	EUN
3. KIM, YONG SIK	PRK

WRESTLING MEN 62 KG

1. SMITH, JOHN	USA
2. MOHAMMADIAN, ASGARI	IRI
3. REINOSO MARTINEZ, LAZARO	CUB

WRESTLING

FREE STYLE 74 KG

1. PARK, JANG-SOON	KOR
2. MONDAY, KENNETH D.	USA
3. KHADEM AZGHADI, AMIRIRI REZA	

SINCHRONIZED SWIMMING

SYNCHRONIZED SWIMMING

1. USA	192.175
2. CAN	189.394
3. JPN	186.868

SYNCHRONIZED SWIMMING SOLO

1. BABB-SPRAGUE, K.	USA	191.848
2. FRECHETTE, S.	CAN	191.717
3. OKUNO, FUMIKO	JPN	187.056

CANOEING

MEN C-1 1000 M

1. BOUKHALOV, NIKOLAI	BUL	4:05.92
2. KLEMENTJEVS, IVANS	LAT	4:06.60
3. ZALA, GYORGY	HUN	4:07.35

CANOEING MEN K-4 1000 M

1. GER	2:54.18
2. HUN	2:54.82
3. AUS	2:56.97

CANOEING MEN K-2 1000 M

1. GER	3:16.10
2. SWE	3:17.70
3. POL	3:18.86

CANOEING MEN C-2 1000 M

1. GER	3:37.42
2. DEN	3:39.26
3. FRA	3:39.51

CANOEING MEN K-1 1000 M

1. ROBINSON, CLINT D.	AUS	3:37.26
2. HOLMANN, KNUT	NOR	3:37.50
3. BARTON, GREG	USA	3:37.93

CANOEING MEN K-1 500 M

1. FIN	1:40.34
2. HUN	1:40.64
3. NOR	1:40.71

CANOEING MEN K-2 500 M

1. GER	1:28.27
2. POL	1:29.84
3. ITA	1:30.00

CANOEING MEN C-1 500 M

1. BUL	1:51.15
2. EUN	1:51.40
3. GER	1:53.00

CANOEING MEN C-2 500 M

1. EUN	1:41.54
2. GER	1:41.68
3. BUL	1:41.94

CANOEING WOMEN K-4 500 M

1. HUN	1:38.32
2. GER	1:38.47
3. SWE	1:39.79

CANOEING WOMEN K-1 500 M

1. GER	1:51.60
2. HUN	1:51.96
3. POL	1:52.36

CANOEING WOMEN K-2 500 M

1. GER	1:40.29
2. SWE	1:40.41
3. HUN	1:40.81

BASKETBALL

MEN

1. USA	
2. CRO	
3. LTU	

WOMEN

1. EUN	
2. CHN	
3. USA	

ATHLETICS

MEN MARATHON

1. HWANG, YOUNG-CHO	KOR	2:13:23
2. MORISHITA, KOICHI	JPN	2:13:45
3. FREIGANG, STEPHAN TIMO	GER	2:14:00

MEN JAVELIN

1. ZELEZNY, JAN	TCH	89.66
2. RATY, SEPPO	FIN	86.60
3. BACKLEY, STEVE	GBR	83.38

MEN 4 x 400 M

1. USA	2:55.74WR
2. CUB	2:59.51
3. GBR	2:59.73

MEN 4 x 100 M

1. USA	37.40WR
2. NIGERIA	37.98
3. CUBA	38.00

MEN 5000 M

1. BAUMANN, DIETER	GER	13:12.52
2. BITOK, PAUL	KEN	13:12.71
3. BAYISA, FITA	ETH	13:13.03

ATHLETICS MEN 1500 M

1. CACHO RUIZ, FERMIN	ESP	3:40.12
2. EL-BASIR, RACHID	MAR	3:40.62
3. SULAIMAN, MOHAMED AHMED	QAT	3:40.69

ATHLETICS MEN LONG JUMP

1. LEWIS, CARL	USA	8.67
2. POWELL, MIKE	USA	8.64
3. GREENE, JOE	USA	8.34

ATHLETICS MEN 400 M HURDLES

1. YOUNG, KEVIN	USA	46.78WR
2. GRAHAM, WINTHROP	JAM	47.66
3. AKABUSI, KRISS	GBR	47.82

ATHLETICS MEN 50 KM WALK

1. PERLOV, ANDREY	EUN	3:50:13
2. MERCENARIO, C.	MEX	3:52:09
3. WEIGEL, RONALD	GER	3:53:45

ATHLETICS MEN POLE VAULT

1. TARASSOV, MAXIM	EUN	5.80
2. TRANDENKOV, I.	EUN	5.80
3. GARCIA, JAVIER	ESP	5.75

ATHLETICS WOMEN 4 x 400 M

1. UNIFIED TEAM	3:20.20
2. USA	3:20.92
3. GBR	3:24.23

ATHLETICS WOMEN 200 M

1. TORRENCE, GWEN	USA	21.81
2. CUTHBERT, JULIET	JAM	22.02
3. OTTEY, MERLENE	JAM	22.09

ATHLETICS WOMEN 100 M HURDLES

1. PATOULIDOU, PARASKEVI	GRE	12.64
2. MARTIN, LA VONNA	USA	12.69
3. DONKOVA, YORDANKA	BUL	12.70

ATHLETICS WOMEN 10000 M

1. TULU, DERARTU	ETH	31:06.02
2. MEYER, ELANA	RSA	31:11.75
3. JENNINGS, LYNN	USA	31:19.89

Barcelona'92

ATHLETICS MEN 200 M

1. MARSH, MIKE	USA	20.01
2. FREDERICKS, FRANK	NAM	20.13
3. BATES, MICHAEL	USA	20.38

ATHLETICS DECATHLON AFTER 7 EVENTS

1. ZMELIK, ROBERT	TCH	6183
2. PEÑALVER, A.	ESP	6122
3. MEIER, PAUL	GER	6041

MEN 3000 M STEEPLECHASE

1. BIRIR, MATHEW	KEN	8:08.84
2. SANG, PATRICK	KEN	8:09.55
3. MUTWOL, WILLIAM	KEN	8:10.74

ATHLETICS WOMEN HIGH JUMP

1. HENKEL, HEIKE	GER	2.02
2. ASTAFEI, GALINA	ROM	2.00
3. QUINTERO, J.	CUB	1.97

ATHLETICS WOMEN 4 x 100 M

1. USA	42.11
2. UNIFIED TEAM	42.16
3. NIGERIA	42.81

ATHLETICS WOMEN 1500 M

1. BOULMERKA, HASSIBA	ALG	3:55.30
2. ROGACHEVA, LYUDMILA	EUN	3:56.91
3. QU, YUNXIA	CHN	3:57.08

ATHLETICS WOMEN HIGH JUMP

1. HENKEL, HEIKE	GER	2.02
2. ASTAFEI, GALINA	ROM	2.00
3. QUINTERO, J.	CUB	1.97

ATHLETICS WOMEN SHOT PUT

1. KRIVELEVA, S.	EUN	21.06
2. HUANG, ZHIHONG	CHN	20.47
3. NEIMKE, KATHRIN	GER	19.78

DIVING

MEN PLATFORM 10 M

1. SUN, SHUWEI	CHN	677.310
2. DONIE, SCOTT R.	USA	633.630
3. XIONG, NI	CHN	600.150

WOMEN SPRINGBOARD 3 m

1. GAO, MIN	CHN	572.400
2. LACHKO, IRINA	EUN	514.140
3. BALDUS, BRITA PIA	GER	503.070

BADMINTON

MEN SINGLES

1. KUSUMA, A.	INA
2. WIRANATA, ARDY	INA

MEN DOUBLES

1. KIM, M./PARK, J.	KOR
2. HARTONO/GUNAWAN	INA

WOMEN SINGLES

1. SUSANTI, SUSI	INA
2. BANG, SOO HYUN	KOR

WOMEN DOUBLES

1. HWANG, H./CHUNG, S.	KOR
2. GUAN, W./NONG, Q.	CHN

ARCHERY

MEN INDIVIDUAL

1. FLUTE, SEBASTIEN	FRA	542
2. CHUNG, JAE-HUN	KOR	542*
3. TERRY, SIMON	GBR	528

MEN TEAMS

1. ESP
2. FIN
3. GBR

WOMEN INDIVIDUAL

1. CHO, YOUN-JEONG	KOR
2. KIM, SOO-NYUNG	KOR
3. VALEEVA, NATALIA	EUN

WOMEN TEAMS

1. KOR
2. CHN
3. EUN

CYCLING

MEN 1 km TIME TRIAL

1. MORENO, JOSE	ESP	1:03.342 UOR
2. KELLY, S.	AUS	1:04.288
3. HARTWELL, ERIN	USA	1:04.753

MEN IND. PURSUIT

1. BOARDMAN, C.	GBR
2. LEHMANN, JENS	GER
3. ANDERSON, G.	NZL

MEN IND. SPRINT

1. FIEDLER, JENS	GER
2. NEIWAND, G.	AUS
3. HARNETT, CURTIS	CAN

MEN IND. ROAD 194 km

1. CASARTELLI, F.	ITA	4:35:21
2. DEKKER, HENDRIK	NED	4:35:22
3. OZOLS, D.	LAT	4:35:24

CYCLING / MEN ROAD TEAM TIME TRIAL

1. GERMANY	GER
2. ITALY	ITA
3. FRANCE	FRA

WOMEN IND. ROAD 81 km

1. WATT, KATHRYN	AUS	2:04:42
2. LONGO-CIPRELLI	FRA	2:05:02
3. KNOL, MONIQUE	NED	2:05:03

WOMEN IND. SPRINT

1. SALUMAE, ERIKA	EST
2. NEUMANN, ANNETT	GER
3. HARINGA, INGRID	NED

MEN 50 k POINTS RACE

1. LOMBARDI, G.	ITA	44
2. VAN BON, LEON	NED	43
3. MATHY, CEDRIC	BEL	41

WOMEN 3 km IND. PURSUIT

1. ROSSNER, PETRA	GER	3:41.753
2. WATT, KATHRYN	AUS	3:43.438

SHOOTING

SHOOTING MEN FREE PISTOL

1. LOUKACHIK, KONSTANTINE	EUN	658.0
2. WANG, YIFU	CHN	657.0
3. SKANAKER, RAGNAR	SWE	657.0

SHOOTING MEN RIFLE

1. FEDKINE, IOURI	EUN	695.3NFOR
2. BADIOU, FRANCK	FRA	691.9
3. RIEDERER, JOHANN	GER	691.7

MEN AIR PISTOL

1. WANG, YIFU	CHN	654.8NFOR
2. PYJIANOV, S.	EUN	684.1
3. BABII, SORIN	ROM	684.1

OPEN EVENTS SKEET

1. ZHANG, SHAN	CHN	223NFOR
2. GIHA YARUR, JUAN JORGE	PER	222
3. ROSSETTI, BRUNO MARIO	ITA	222

MEN SB RIFLE, PRONE

1. LEE, EUN-CHUL	KOR	702.5NFOR
2. STENVAAG, HARALD	NOR	701.4
3. PLETIKOSIC, S.	IOP	701.1

MEN RAPID-FIRE PISTOL

1. SCHUMANN, RALF	GER	885NFOR
2. KUZMINS, A.	LAT	882
3. VOKHMIANINE, V.	EUN	882

MEN SB RIFLE, 3 POS.

1. PETIKIANE, G.	EUN	1267.4NFOR
2. FOTH, ROBERT	USA	1266.6
3. KOBA, RYOHEI	JPN	1265.9

MEN 10 M RUNNING TARGET

1. JAKOSITS, M.	GER	673NFOR
2. ASRABAEV, A.	EUN	672
3. RACANSKY, LUBOS	TCH	670

OPEN EVENTS TRAP FINAL

1. HRDLICKA, PETR	TCH	
2. WATANABE, KAZUMI	JPN	
3. VENTURINI, MARCO	ITA	

WOMEN AIR RIFLE

1. YEO, KAB-SOON	KOR	498.2NFOR
2. LETCHEVA, VESELA	BUL	495.3
3. BINDER, ARANKA	IOP	495.1

SHOOTING WOMEN SPORT PISTOL

1. LOGVINENKO, MARINA	EUN	684.0NFOR
2. LI, DUIHONG	CHN	680.0
3. MUNKHBAYAR, DORZHSUREN	MGL	679.0

WOMEN SB RIFLE, 3 POS.

1. MEILI, LAUNI	USA	684.3NFOR
2. MATOVA, NONKA	BUL	682.7
3. KSIAZKIEWICZ, M.	POL	681.5

WOMEN AIR PISTOL

1. LOGVINENKO, M.	EUN	486.4NFOR
2. SEKARIC, JASNA	IOP	486.4NFOR
3. GROUSDEVA, MARIA	BUL	481.6

ROWING

MEN COXED FOURS

1. ROM	5:59.37
2. GER	6:00.34
3. POL	6:03.27

MEN 2 x; DOUBLE SCULLS

1. HAWKINS, STEPHEN MARK ANTONIE PETER	AUS	6:17.32
2. JONKE, ARNOLD ZERBST, CHRISTOPH	AUT	6:18.42
3. ZWOLLE, HENK-JAN RIENKS, NICO	NED	6:22.82

MEN 2-; COXLESS PAIRS

1. REDGRAVE, STEVEN PINSENT, MATTHEW CLIVE	GBR	6:27.72
2. HOELTZENBEIN, PETER J. VON ETTINGSHAUSEN, COLIN	GER	6:32.68
3. COP, IZTOK ZVEGELJ, DENIS	SLO	6:33.43

MEN 1x; SINGLE SCULLS

1. LANGE, THOMAS	GER	6:51.40
2. CHALUPA, VACLAV	TCH	6:52.93
3. BRONIEWSKI, KAJETAN	POL	6:56.82

MEN COXED PAIRS

1. SEARLE, JONATHAN SEARLE, GREG MARK HERBERT, GARRY GERARD PAU	GBR	6:49.83
2. ABBAGNALE, CARMINE ABBAGNALE, GIUSEPPE DI CAPUA, GIUSEPPE	ITA	6:50.98
3. POPESCU, DIMITRIE TAGA, NICOLAIE RADUCANU, DUMITRU	ROM	6:51.58

MEN COXLESS FOURS

1. AUS	5:55.04
2. USA	5:56.68
3. SLO	5:58.24

MEN QUADRUPLE SCULLS

1. GER	5:45.17
2. NOR	5:47.09
3. ITA	5:47.33

MEN COXED EIGHTS

1. CAN	5:29.53
2. ROM	5:29.67
3. GER	5:31.00

WOMEN COXLESS FOURS

1. CAN	1.6:30.85
2. USA	6:31.86
3. GER	6:32.34

WOMEN DOUBLE SCULLS

1. KOEPPEN, KERSTIN BORON, KATHRIN	GER	6:49.00
2. COCHELEA, VERONICA LIPA, ELISABETA	ROM	6:51.47
3. GU, XIAOLI LU, HUALI	CHN	6:55.16

WOMEN COXLESS PAIRS

1. MCBEAN, MARNIE ELIZA- BETH HEDDLE, KATHLEEN	CAN	7:06.22
2. WERREMEIER, STEFANI SCHWERZMANN, INGEBURG	GER	7:07.96
3. SEATON, ANNA B. PIERSON, STEPHANIE MAXWEL	USA	7:08.11

WOMEN SINGLE SCULLS

1. LIPA, ELISABETA	ROM	7:25.54
2. BREDAEL, ANNELIES	BEL	7:26.64
3. LAUMANN, SILKEN SUZETTE	CAN	7:28.85

WOMEN QUADRUPLE SCULLS

1. GER	6:20.18
2. ROM	6:24.34
3. EUN	6:25.07

WOMEN COXED EIGHTS

1. CAN	
2. ROM	
3. GER	

JUDO

MEN + 95 kg

1. KHAKHALEICHVILI, DAVID	EUN	
2. OGAWA, NAOYA	JPN	
3. DOUILLET, DAVID	FRA	

MEN - 95 kg

1. KOVACS, ANTAL	HUN	
2. STEVENS, RAYMOND	GBR	
3. MEIJER, THEO	NED	

JUDO MEN - 86 kg

1. LEGIEN, WALDEMAR	POL	
2. TAYOT, PASCAL	FRA	
3. OKADA, HIROTAKA	JPN	

— You've drilled beneath the earth and under oceans. Where will it all stop ?

— I don't know, but wherever it is, we'll be there.

If you want to tell the story of ELF, you have to talk a little geography. Over the years, on every continent, beneath every ocean, ELF has explored for oil and gas. Thanks to its discoveries the group has become one of the world's ten largest oil companies. And the men and women who work for ELF will never stop exploring. In fact, if you ask them where their search might end, they'll smile and tell you that the earth isn't the only planet in the solar system. ■

OUR DEDICATION GOES FURTHER

JUDO MEN - 78 kg

1. YOSHIDA, HIDEHIKO	JPN	
2. MORRIS, JASON N.	USA	
3. DAMAISIN, BERTRAND	FRA	

JUDO MEN LIGHTWEIGHT

1. KOGA, TOSHIHIKO	JPN	
2. HAJTOS, BERTALAN	HUN	
3. CHUNG, HOON	KOR	

JUDO MEN HALF-LIGHTWEIGHT

1. SAMPAIO CARDOSO, ROGERIO	BRA	
2. CSAK, JOZSEF	HUN	
3. QUELLMALZ, UDO GUNTER	GER	

JUDO MEN EXTRA LIGHTWEIGHT

1. GOUSSEINOV, NAZIM	EUN	
2. YOON, HYUN	KOR	
3. TRAUTMANN, RICHARD	GER	

JUDO

1. ZHUANG, XIAOYAN	CHN	
2. RODRIGUEZ VILLANUEVA, ESTELA	CUB	
3. LUPINO, NATALIA	FRA	

JUDO WOMEN - 72 kg

1. KIM, MI-JUNG	KOR	
2. TANABE, YOKO	JPN	
3. DE KOK, IRENE	NED	

JUDO WOMEN - 66 kg

1. REVE JIMENEZ, ODALIS	CUB	
2. PIERANTOZZI, EMANUELA	ITA	
3. RAKELS, HEIDI	BEL	

JUDO WOMEN - 61 kg

1. FLEURY, CATHERINE	FRA	
2. ARAD, YAEL	ISR	
3. ZHANG, DI	CHN	

JUDO WOMEN LIGHTWEIGHT

1. BLASCO SOTO, MIRIAM	ESP	
2. FAIRBROTHER, NICOLA KIM	GBR	
3. GONZALEZ MORALES, DRIULIS	CUB	

JUDO WOMEN HALF-LIGHTWEIGHT

1. MUÑOZ MARTINEZ, ALMUDENA	ESP	
2. MIZOGUCHI, NORIKO	JPN	
3. LI, ZHONGYUN	CHN	
3. RENDLE, SHARON SUSAN	GBR	

JUDO WOMEN EXTRA LIGHTWEIGHT

1. NOWAK, CECILE	FRA	
2. TAMURA, RYOKO	JPN	
3. SENYURT, HULYA	TUR	

SWIMMING

MEN 50 M FREESTYLE

1. POPOV, ALEXANDRE	EUN	21.91NOR
2. BIONDI, MATTHEW N.	USA	22.09
3. JAGER, TOM M.	USA	22.30

MEN 100 M FREESTYLE

1. POPOV, ALEXANDRE	EUN	49.02
2. BORGES, GUSTAVO	BRA	49.43
3. CARON, STEPHAN	FRA	49.50

MEN 200 M FREESTYLE

1. SADOVYI, EVGUENI	EUN	1:46.70NOR
2. HOLMERTZ, ANDERS	SWE	1:46.86
3. KASVIO, ANTTI ALEXANDER	FIN	1:47.63

MEN 400 M FREESTYLE

1. SADOVYI, EVGUENI	EUN	3:45.00NWR
2. PERKINS, KIEREN JOHN	AUS	3:45.16
3. HOLMERTZ, ANDERS	SWE	3:46.77

MEN 1500 M FREESTYLE

1. PERKINS, KIEREN JOHN	AUS	14:43.48NWR
2. HOUSMAN, GLEN CLIFFORD	AUS	14:55.29
3. HOFFMANN, JOERG	GER	15:02.29

MEN 4x100 M FREESTYLE

1. USA		3:16.74
2. EUN		3:17.56
3. GER		3:17.90

MEN 4x200 M FREESTYLE

1. EUN		7:19.95NWR
2. SWE		7:15.51
3. USA		7:16.23

MEN 100 M BACKSTROKE

1. TEWKSBURY, MARK	CAN	53.98NOR
2. ROUSE, JEFF NORMAN	USA	54.04
3. BERKOFF, DAVID C.	USA	54.78

SWIMMING MEN 200 M BACKSTROKE

1. LOPEZ-ZUBERO, MARTIN	ESP	1:58.47NOR
2. SELKOV, VLADIMIR	EUN	1:58.87
3. BATTISTELLI, STEFANO	ITA	1:59.40

MEN 100 M BREASTSTROKE

1. DIEBEL, NELSON W.	USA	1:01.50NOR
2. ROZSA, NORBERT	HUN	1:01.68
3. ROGERS, PHILIP JOHN	AUS	1:01.76

MEN 200 M BREASTSTROKE

1. BARROWMAN, MIKE	USA	2:10.16NWR
2. ROZSA, NORBERT	HUN	2:11.23
3. GILLINGHAM, NICK	GBR	2:11.29

MEN 100 M BUTTERFLY

1. MORALES, PABLO	USA	53.32
2. SZUKALA, RAFAL	POL	53.35
3. NESTY, ANTHONY CONRAD	SUR	53.41

MEN 200 M BUTTERFLY

1. STEWART, MEL	USA	1:56.26NOR
2. LOADER, DANYON JOSEPH	NZL	1:57.93
3. ESPOSITO, FRANCK	FRA	1:58.51

MEN 200 M MEDLEY

1. DARNYI, TAMAS	HUN	2:00.76
2. BURGESS, GREGORY S.	USA	2:00.97
3. CZENE, ATTILA	HUN	2:01.00

MEN 400 M MEDLEY

1. DARNYI, TAMAS	HUN	4:14.23NOR
2. NAMESNIK, ERIC	USA	4:15.57
3. SACCHI, LUCA	ITA	4:16.34

MEN 4x100 M MEDLEY

1. USA		3:36.93EWR
2. EUN		3:38.56
3. CAN		3:39.66

WOMEN 50 M FREESTYLE

1. YANG, WENYI	CHN	24.79NWR
2. ZHUANG, YONG	CHN	25.08
3. MARTINO, ANGEL	USA	25.23

WOMEN 100 M FREESTYLE

1. ZHUANG, YONG	CHN	54.65NOR
2. THOMPSON, JENNIFER B	USA	54.84
3. VAN ALMSICK, FRANZISKA	GER	54.94

SWIMMING WOMEN 200 M FREESTYLE

1. HAISLETT, NICOLE L.	USA	1:57.90
2. VAN ALMSICK, FRANZISKA	GER	1:58.00
3. KIELGASS, KERSTIN	GER	1:59.67

WOMEN 400 M FREESTYLE

1. HASE, DAGMAR	GER	4:07.18
2. EVANS, JANET B.	USA	4:07.37
3. LEWIS, HAYLEY JANE	AUS	4:11.22

WOMEN 800 M FREESTYLE

1. EVANS, JANET B.	USA	8:25.52
2. LEWIS, HAYLEY JANE	AUS	8:30.34
3. HENKE, JANA	GER	8:30.99

WOMEN 4x100 M FREESTYLE

1. USA		3:39.46NWR
2. CHN		3:40.12
3. GER		3:41.60

WOMEN 100 M BACKSTROKE

1. EGERSZEGI, KRISZTINA	HUN	1:00.68NOR
2. SZABO, TUNDE	HUN	1:01.14
3. LOVELESS, LEA E.	USA	1:01.43

WOMEN 200 M BACKSTROKE

1. EGERSZEGI, KRISZTINA	HUN	2:07.06NOR
2. HASE, DAGMAR	GER	2:09.46
3. STEVENSON, NICOLE DAWN	AUS	2:10.20

WOMEN 100 M BREASTSTROKE

1. ROUDKOVSKAIA, ELENA	EUN	1:08.00
2. NALL, ANITA L.	USA	1:08.17
3. RILEY, SAMANTHA LINETTE	AUS	1:09.25

WOMEN 200 M BREASTSTROKE

1. IWASAKI, KYOKO	JPN	2:26.65NOR
2. LIN, LI	CHN	2:26.85
3. NALL, ANITA	USA	2:26.88

WOMEN 100 M BUTTERFLY

1. QIAN, HONG	CHN	58.62NOR
2. AHMANN-LEIGHTON, CHRISTINE	USA	58.74
3. PLEWINSKI, CATHERINE	FRA	59.01

WOMEN 200 M BUTTERFLY

1. SANDERS, SUMMER E.	USA	2:08.67
2. WANG, XIAOHONG	CHN	2:09.01
3. O'NEILL, SUSAN	AUS	2:09.03

WOMEN 200 M MEDLEY

1. LIN, LI	CHN	2:11.65NWR
2. SANDERS, SUMMER E.	USA	2:11.91
3. HUNGER, DANIELA	GER	2:13.92

WOMEN 400 M MEDLEY

1. EGERSZEGI, KRISZTINA	HUN	4:36.54
2. LIN, LI	CHN	4:36.73
3. SANDERS, SUMMER E.	USA	4:37.58

WOMEN 4x100 MEDLEY

1. USA		4:02.54NWR
2. GER		4:05.19
3. EUN		4:06.44

DIVING

WOMEN PLATFORM 10 m

1. FU, MINGXIA	CHN	461.430
2. MIROCHINA, ELENA	EUN	411.630
3. CLARK, MARY ELLEN	USA	401.910

MEN SPRINGBOARD 3 m

1. LENZI, MARK EDWARD	USA	676.530
2. TAN LIANGDE	CHN	645.570
3. SAOUTINE, DMITRI	EUN	627.780

MODERN PENTATHLON

INDIVIDUAL

1. SKRZYPASZEK, A.	POL	5559
2. MIZSER, ATTILA	HUN	5446
3. ZENOVKA, EDOUARD	EUN	5361

TEAMS

1. POL	16018
2. EUN	15924
3. ITA	15760

Official Sponsor of the 1992
Olympic Summer Games
Barcelona'92

Official Sponsor of the 1992
United States Olympic Team
USA

Official Sponsor of the
European Football Championship
UEFA 92

Official Sponsor of the
1994 World Cup
WORLD CUP '94

BRINGING YOU BETTER LIGHT
Because light is life

Philips Lighting

PHILIPS

PHILIPS

More than two million pins are expected to be traded at the Coca Cola Official Olympic Pin Trading Centre, which also plays host to celebrities. Pin trading has become the most popular Olympic spectator sport because it transcends the barriers of language and cultural differences.

I M P R E S S U M

Published by:
IMS/STUDIO 6, Lausanne - Switzerland

IMS/STUDIO 6 thanks the following people for their invaluable help in the preparation of this book, without whom its publication would not have been possible in such a short time.

Director:
Goran A. TAKATCH

Art Director:
Muris CAMO

Designers:
Eric JACQUARD
Sabine ERISMANN

Photography Director:
Carla TRACCANELLA

Production Coordination:
Olivier COULET

Marketing Manager:
Christophe STADLER

Texts:
Stephen WOODWARD

Photography:
IMS/STUDIO 6
Maarten VAN DER ENDE

THE ALLSPORT PHOTOGRAPHIC
OLYMPIC TEAM

Steve POWELL
Tony Duffy
Bob Martin
David Canon
Mike Powell
Simon Bruty
Pascal Rondeau
Chris Cole
Gray Mortimore
Shaun Botterill
Mike Hewitt
Gary Newkirk
Koji Aoki
David Leah
Henry Dobkin
Nathan Bilow

VANDYSTADT (ALLSPORT France)

Gerard VANDYSTADT

Thierry Deketelaere
Yann Guichaoua
Bernard Asset
Richard Martin
Frederic Chehu

Special thanks to:

Anne-Lise BORBOEN WACHTER,
IMS/STUDIO 6
Lee MARTIN, ALLSPORT
Michelle IRACHABAL, IOC
Matti SALMENKYLA
Michèle VERDIER, IOC
Stéphane KEMPINAIRE, VANDYSTADT
James MARKLAND, PROFESSIONAL TEAM
PUBLICATIONS.
And all the team from Grafos SA for its kindness
and professionalism.

Color separation:

FOTOINFORMATICA SA (Barcelona, Spain)

Printing:

GRAFOS SA Arte Sobre el Papel
(Barcelona, Spain)

All photographs in the book were taken exclusively on Kodak films and processed in Kodak laboratories in the Main Press Center Barcelona '92.

USA - EDITION
100,000 copies published by
PROFESSIONAL TEAM PUBLICATIONS, Inc.
21 Charles Street, Westport, CT 06880 / Tel.: (203) 227 1775